THERMOS

QUALITY SINCE 1907

GAS GRILL
Cookbook

Editor-in-Chief:	*Terry L. Firkins*
Writer & Food Editor:	*Jeanette G. White*
Home Economist:	*Patricia J. Schmeling*
Administrative Assistant:	*Laurie A. Marzahl*
Art & Design:	*Barbara Boehler*
Photography:	*Scott Ritenour, Milwaukee*
Typography:	*Ries Graphics, Milwaukee*
Lithography:	*Schilffarth & Kress, Milwaukee*
Project Director:	*James M. Fitzgerald*

Library of Congress Catalog Card Number: 89-081039

ISBN: 0-87502-240-5

Second printing: November 1992

CONTENTS

GREAT GAS GRILLING

Any season is barbecue season when you're grilling with gas! You get all the pleasure and excitement of outdoor cooking without the fuss and mess associated with charcoal grilling. No need to replenish the charcoal supply constantly . . . a tank of propane gas will last a long time, even with daily use. No long delays waiting for the coals to reach the right temperature . . . your gas grill starts with the push of a button or the light of a match and is ready for use in minutes. No erratic grilling and out-of-control flare-ups . . . the heat source is constant and even and easy to control. Your gas grill is also economical to operate. Summer, winter, or in between, whether the temperature soars to a hundred in the shade or plummets to zero in the sun, your gas grill will perform to perfection every time.

GET IT TOGETHER!

All gas grills require some assembly by the owner. This may mean a few minutes or a few hours, depending on the complexity of the particular model and your manual dexterity. Seriously, the work is not complicated. Just follow the procedures outlined in the Instruction Book. Each step is discussed in detail and fully illustrated. You will need a few basic tools: an adjustable wrench, Phillips and regular tip screwdrivers, a pair of pliers, and a hammer. (A muffin pan or divided tray is a great asset for sorting and keeping track of the small parts, screws, and nuts needed during assembly.) Now you can enjoy years of carefree outdoor cooking on your gas grill.

WHICH PART DOES WHAT?

Now that the grill is together and ready to use, let's review its major parts and their functions. Many of these parts will be mentioned repeatedly in recipe instructions.

Grill Top — is the hinged metal cover with a glass viewing window, heat indicator, and a fold-away warming grid.

Grill Bottom — contains the burners, wire grate, lava rocks, and cooking grids.

Burners — are fueled by the propane gas and heat the lava rocks.

Wire Grate — is located in the grill bottom. It supports the lava rocks above the burners, allowing heat from the gas to circulate freely around the rocks.

Lava Rocks — are pure volcanic rocks that absorb and retain heat efficiently, ensuring a steady even heat at a reliable temperature.

Cooking Grids — are the surface on which most grilling or cooking is performed. Food may be placed directly on the grids or in pans or skillets placed on the grids. Depending on the model, your grill may have one or two grids.

Cart — supports the grill and contains the control panel, a pan or platform for the propane gas tank, and shelves (front, left, and right) for food and equipment. The wheels allow the grill to be rolled with ease from place to place.

Control Panel — contains step-by-step instructions for starting the grill; controls for adjusting the grill burners (HI, MED, LO, and OFF); and a fuel gauge which indicates the amount of gas in your propane tank.

Valve, Hose, & Regulator Assembly — connects the burners to the gas supply. The regulator fitting has left-handed threads; therefore, it must be turned counterclockwise to attach it to the propane tank valve. Always turn off the propane tank valve when the grill is not in use.

WHERE'S THE HEAT?

Your gas grill is fueled by propane gas, which is also known as LP gas, or liquefied petroleum. A device called a venturi, which is similar to the carburetor on your car, controls the amount of air that mixes with the propane. This process provides a gas very similar to the natural gas that operates conventional appliances, such as ovens and furnaces. Lighting the burners produces the same efficient blue flame as that of a gas range. The lava rocks scattered across the grate are heated by the flame from the burners during the preheat period. The hot rocks, in turn, heat the grill and cook the food on the grids or rotisserie.

The propane tank for your grill is always shipped empty and must be filled by a reputable dealer. At the factory, compressed air is used in testing the empty tank. Some of this air may remain and must be expelled before the tank is filled with propane for the first time. Alert the dealer that the tank is new and has not been used.

Like any petroleum-based product, propane is a safe and reliable fuel if used properly. It should be stored as you would gasoline for the lawn mower. When not in regular use, the ideal place to store the propane tank is outdoors in a well ventilated area, away from direct sunlight or heat. Do not store it in the basement, garage, or any other building. Actually, you can keep the grill, with the tank connected, right on your patio the year 'round ready to use at any time. Just remember to close the tank valve after each use. Now for a few suggestions and safeguards!

Basic Instructions: Before using the grill, be sure to read the guidelines in the Instruction Book packed with your unit. Whenever you have a question or problem, simply check that manual. It offers a variety of essential and helpful information.

Leak Test: Run the Leak Test before using your grill for the first time, after storing the grill for a long period, and every time the propane tank is refilled or reconnected to the grill. (Follow the quick step-by-step procedure outlined in your Instruction Book.) *Never* check for leaks with a lighter or lighted match.

Hose Assembly: Inspect the assembly each time before using the grill.

Gas Leaks: If you smell gas, shut off the gas supply at the tank valve, extinguish any open flame, and open the grill top. If the odor continues, immediately have your gas supplier check the tank.

Combustibles: Maintain a 3-foot clearance, in every direction, between your grill and any combustible material.

Tank Plug: When the propane tank is not connected to the grill, be sure the valve is closed and the "P.O.L." or cylinder plug is inserted in the valve. The tank must be stored in an upright position.

LET'S GRILL!

You are now well acquainted with the fundamentals of your gas grill. So, it's time for the fun . . . let's get grilling! Before grilling for the first time, let the grill heat on high for at least 30 minutes or until no paint odor remains. Here are the basic steps to follow every time you grill:

- Open the grill top.

- Check the gas gauge to be sure you have enough propane; then, turn on the gas supply at the tank valve. When the gauge registers 1/4 full, it is time to refill your propane tank.

- Remove the cooking grids from the grill.

- Be sure the lava rocks are spread in an even layer over the grate.

- Turn the right control knob to high (HI) and quickly press and release the igniter button. The right burner should light immediately. If it doesn't, turn the control knob to off and try again in 5 minutes. For grills that do not have an automatic igniter, simply insert a lighted match through the lighting hole.

- Preheat the grill by turning the left control to high, closing the grill top, and leaving both controls on high for 5 minutes. This step is essential for heating the lava rocks, which must be hot enough to radiate cooking heat.

- Turn the controls to the temperature designated in the recipe, or follow these general guidelines: *high* heat for preheating the grill and searing meat; *medium to low* for grilling meat and poultry; and *medium-low to low* for seafood, fruit, and vegetables. Depending on the amount of food to be grilled, only one grid may be needed. In this case, turn off the burner under the other grid to conserve fuel.

- Return the grids to the grill and lightly brush them with vegetable oil. This will prevent food from sticking to the grids.

- Place the food on the grids and close the grill top. Now you're grilling! Just follow the recipe directions for marinating and brushing the food with basting sauce.

- To shut down the grill, turn off both the burners and the gas supply.

Though the most efficient and controlled grilling is accomplished with the grill top closed, it is possible to grill with the top open. This method is impractical for large cuts of meat or whole chickens and turkeys, as the cooking time will be considerably longer. It is easier to control the doneness of steaks, chops, hamburgers, frankfurters, and similarly sized foods with the grill top open, and the difference in grilling time will be negligible. The choice is yours!

CHECK THE TECHNIQUES!

There are two basic techniques for gas grilling. Selecting the right one is simply a matter of deciding whether you need a heat source directly under the food (**Direct Method**) or away from the food (**Indirect Method**).

DIRECT METHOD: This method is generally the choice for grilling meat, sautéing food in a skillet, stir-frying, and similar cooking procedures. For example, the direct method is the one you'll use to grill steaks and chops, cook roasts on a rotisserie, heat sauces, and roast potatoes or corn. With the grill top closed, meat will absorb the smoky flavor created by the fat dripping on the lava rocks.

INDIRECT METHOD: To cook by this technique, turn on one burner, but place the food on the opposite grid. Select this method when you want to simulate the cooking environment of a traditional oven. It is the method used for keeping foods warm and for baking casseroles, breads, cakes, and pies. Indirect cooking also can be done by placing food on the Warming Grid, if your grill has one.

You will often use both methods simultaneously. For example, you may be grilling chicken on one grid, while a vegetable or bread is warming on the other grid over the unlit burner.

Searing is another technique you may use frequently. The result is juicier steaks and roasts. To sear meat, preheat the grill on high for 5 minutes; then place the meat on the grids or rotisserie. Close the grill top for 1 to 3 minutes. (Meat on the grids should be turned after 2 minutes.) This procedure will brown the outside of the meat and seal in the juices. Next, open the grill top, turn the controls to the cooking temperature designated in a recipe, and let the grill cool. Once the correct temperature is reached, close the grill top and proceed with your grilling or roasting.

CONTROL FLARE-UPS!

When fat or basting sauces drip on the lava rocks, flare-ups, or flames beneath the food, will likely occur. In some situations a very limited amount of flare-up may be desirable, as it will produce a smoky flavor and will also sear the meat. However, large or sustained flare-ups can pose definite problems, especially for the inexperienced. These tips can help prevent or control flare-ups:

- Trim excess fat from meat before grilling.

- Grill with the grill top closed.

- Place a drip pan on the lava rocks or grate under any food that has a considerable amount of fat.

- Reduce heat and rearrange the food if there is too much flame.

- Do not let too much grease accumulate on the lava rocks. Use the "burn-off" cleaning method each time you grill.

- Check the grease drain hole to assure it is not clogged.

Soak wood chips in water before use in wood chip logs or Thermos® Grill Smoker.

Form drained wood chips into a log and wrap in foil.

SMOKE THAT MEAT!

If you enjoy the enticing aroma and tantalizing flavor of smokehouse grilling, toss a few wood chips on the lava rocks. This will produce a mild smoked flavor. However, if you want a more intense flavor, the process requires a little more effort. First select the wood of your choice. There are many types available. Hickory, mesquite, apple wood, natural cherry, and maple are a few favorites. Next:

- Soak 3 cups of wood chips in water as directed on the package.

- Shape the chips into a log.

Place the log directly on the lava rocks. A drip pan with water provides moisture, where desirable.

- Place the log on a sheet of foil. Bring the long sides of the foil together at the top; then, double fold the sides and ends.

- Puncture the foil in several places to allow the smoke to escape.

- To provide moisture, move the lava rocks to the left side of the grate. Place a drip pan filled with 2 inches of water on the right side.

- Remove the cooking grids and preheat the grill on high for 5 minutes. Place wood chip log on the rocks. Close the grill top and heat 10 to 20 minutes or until the chips begin to smolder. Return the grids to the grill and brush them with oil.

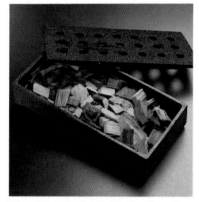

The Thermos® Grill Smoker is a handy alternative to a wood chip log.

- Turn the right control to off and the left control to low. Place the food to be smoked on the right grid or on the rotisserie.

- Close the grill top and let the food smoke for about 3 to 6 hours. Check the grill each hour and replace the log as needed.

An easy alternative to the wood chip log is the Thermos® Grill Smoker. This is a small cast-iron box with holes in the cover to allow the smoke to escape and flavor the food. To use, simply fill the smoker with soaked wood chips and place it on the lava rocks. Let the chips smolder before placing food on the grill.

Tie a rolled roast in several places.

Rotisserie cooking is effortless with a gas grill.

Push the spit rod lengthwise through the center of the roast.

Press holding fork tines into roast and tighten thumb screws.

ROAST IT ON YOUR ROTISSERIE!

A rotisserie is one of the most useful grill accessories. It allows large cuts of meat or whole chickens, turkey, or fish to brown and cook evenly and more quickly than grilling directly on the grids. There are three types of Thermos® rotisseries available . . . cordless, electric, and the deluxe model, which operates on either batteries or electricity. Battery-driven rotisseries have the flexibility to move with the grill to any location. The electric model never needs recharging. The deluxe model combines the best attributes of both units. Assemble and install your rotisserie according to the instructions included with the particular model.

Roasting on a rotisserie does require a little advance preparation. After removing the meat, poultry, or fish from the refrigerator, let the food stand about 30 to 60 minutes to reach room temperature. (This will firm the food and ensure even cooking.) Many foods, such as rolled roasts and whole poultry or fish, should be tied in several places with heavy string to maintain a more uniform shape and to prevent legs and wings from dragging across the lava rocks.

Slip the spit rod collar onto the spit rod next to the wooden handle. Then slide one fork (tines pointing away from the collar) onto the rod. Insert the spit rod lengthwise through the food. Slide the remaining fork onto the rod and press the tines of both forks into the food. Center the food on the spit rod and tighten the thumb screws. Check the balance by rotating the rods in your hands. If one side feels heavy, reposition the food until it is balanced.

To prepare the grill, remove the cooking grids. Place the drip pan on the lava rocks in the center of the grill. For a moist heat, fill the pan with water to a 2-inch depth. Preheat the grill on high for 5 minutes. Then position the spit rod and operate the rotisserie according to the instructions for your specific model. Spit-roast the food as your recipe directs. A flat rotisserie basket and a chicken/rib basket are handy accessories for spit-roasting smaller-sized foods on the rotisserie.

ACCESSORIZE YOUR GRILL!

A wide variety of helpful accessories and cooking tools are available for you and your gas grill. The following accessories may be purchased at your nearest dealer or by ordering through the Thermos® toll-free number **1-800-323-1255**.

Ceramic Briquettes — These can be substituted for the lava rocks. They heat quickly, distribute heat more evenly, and minimize flare-ups by absorbing less grease and food particles.

Lava Rocks — Mined from real volcanoes, the rocks burn clean and distribute heat efficiently.

Grill Smoker — The oblong, cast-iron box has holes in the cover to allow smoke from the wood chips to escape and flavor the food. A grill smoker eliminates the need to form wood chips into a log.

Heat Distribution Plate — The specially designed "porcelainized" plates distribute heat evenly, control flare-ups, and eliminate the need for lava rocks and the grate.

Wood Chips — Available in mesquite, natural cherry, hickory wood, cob & maple, and apple wood, the chips add a smoky barbecue flavor to the food.

Rotisseries — Available versions include a cordless, electric, or the deluxe rotisserie, which operates on either battery or electricity and has an AC/DC adaptor.

Rotary Shish-Kabober — The chrome-plated, double-pronged kabober holds meat and vegetables securely as they rotate and cook to a delicious doneness.

Utensil Set — Available in four styles, each set includes a long-handled fork, spatula, and tongs with attractive wooden handles. Long-handled brushes are provided with some sets.

Shish Kabob Set — Six, foot-long skewers rest on a raised rack, which prevents kabobs from sticking to the grids and facilitates turning.

Flat Rotisserie Basket — This versatile chrome-plated basket, with a self-locking lid, holds chops, burgers, steaks, and other foods and can be adjusted to several thicknesses.

Chicken/Rib Basket — Irregularly shaped chicken parts and ribs tumble to an even doneness in this chrome-plated basket, used with the rotisserie.

Hot Dog Rack — Another convenient rotisserie attachment, the 12-prong rack is ideal for frankfurters, brats, and other sausages.

Rib Rack — The hefty divided rack holds ribs in an upright position to reduce the loss of flavorful juices.

Roast/Poultry Rack — The rack raises large roasts, chicken, and turkey above the grids, allowing the heat to circulate freely around the food.

Broiler Basket — The convenient basket has an extra long handle for easy turning and holds anything from steaks, chops, and ribs, to tender chicken and fish.

Fish Broiler — This fish-shaped basket separates whole fish or fillets from the grids and allows easy turning.

Hamburger Broiler — Available in two sizes that hold four or six patties, the wire broiler will let you grill the perfect burger.

Grill Covers — Made of sturdy nylon-reinforced vinyl, the covers are available in two styles. The short version covers the grill top and bottom; the full length style protects the entire grill and cart.

Cleaning Brushes — The following brushes are helpful for keeping your grill in top operating condition: The **Grill Cleaning Brush** is a sturdy brass-bristled brush that is especially effective for cleaning chrome, cast-iron, or porcelain grids. The **Grill Scrub Brush** is a double-duty clean-up tool that has both a scrubber and a brass-bristled brush mounted on a broad grip molded to fit the hand comfortably. The **Porcelain Cleaning Brush** is a specially designed brush which cleans porcelain grids without scratching them. The **Venturi Brush** is designed to clean spider webs and other foreign material from venturi tubes.

Other available accessories include a handy butane lighter, grill shelves, degreaser, hi-temp paint, and an assortment of gourmet barbecue spices and oils.

KEEP IT CLEAN!

For a detailed discussion about the maintenance and storage of your gas grill, check your Instruction Book. On a more regular basis, "burn off" the grease and residue every time you grill:

- Turn both controls to high.

- Close the grill top and allow the grill to burn on high for 15 minutes.

- Open the grill top and allow the grease and residue to burn until the flames subside. (Be alert to flare-ups when opening the grill cover.)

- Turn controls to off position.

- Turn off the gas supply at the propane tank valve and let the grill cool.

For more intensive cleaning, the Clean-Up Kit and other Thermos® cleaning aids can help you do the job right.

GRILL SAFELY!

Here are a few safety guidelines to follow every time you use your gas grill:

- Never leave the grill unattended.
- Instruct children to play at a safe distance from the grill.
- Never light the grill with the top down.
- Avoid touching any metal surface of the grill, as it becomes very hot during operation.
- Use long-handled utensils to manipulate the food on the grill.
- On a windy day, position the grill so that the smoke will blow downwind, away from you and the grill.
- Wear close-fitting clothing or a barbecue apron, as loose clothing could be blown toward the grill and might catch fire.
- Never use the grill indoors. If the grill is stored indoors, disconnect the propane gas tank and store it outdoors. (Check your gas grill Instruction Book for other safety measures.)

GRILLING TERMS YOU SHOULD KNOW!

Barbecue — to roast or broil on a grid or spit, over hot coals or rocks, often basting with a sauce.

Baste — to flavor or moisten food during grilling by brushing with a sauce or liquid.

Drip Pan — a metal or foil pan, placed on the grate or lava rocks to catch drippings.

Flare-Up — sudden high flames that occur when fat drippings or other residue ignite.

Flash Back — fires in and around the venturi tubes caused by clogged venturi tubes which obstruct the gas flow. Should this occur, immediately turn off the gas supply at the tank valve. (Consult your Instruction Book about procedures for inspecting and cleaning the venturi tubes.)

Grill — to roast or broil on grids, over hot coals or rocks.

Marinate — to allow food, especially meat, poultry, or fish, to stand in a well-seasoned sauce or liquid for a specified time to absorb flavor.

Preheat — to heat the grill on high for 5 minutes before cooking.

Roast — to cook meat by dry heat, without moisture.

Rotisserie — a grill apparatus that rotates the spit-rod.

Smoke House Grilling — to grill over smoldering wood chips that smoke and flavor food.

Spit-Roast — to roast on a stationary or revolving spit-rod.

Spit-Rod — a metal rod inserted in food for support on the rotisserie.

Tenderize — to make meat tender by marinating in an acidic liquid, pounding with a meat mallet, or sprinkling with meat tenderizer.

Venturi — a device similar to an automobile carburetor that controls the amount of air mixing with the propane to provide the gas that fuels the burners.

Wood Chip Log — a foil-wrapped "log" of soaked wood chips.

SAUCES, MARINADES, & MORE!

Most barbecue enthusiasts enjoy the extra flavor that marinades, sauces, and seasoned butters add to grilled foods, especially meat, poultry, and seafood. Although advance preparation is minimal, a little advance thinking is needed so that everything will be ready when the grill is hot. When selecting sauces and marinades, here are a few considerations for the novice or reminders for the expert.

FLAVOR: Is the food mild-flavored, strong, or somewhere in between? Select a lightly-seasoned sauce or marinade for mild foods such as seafood, chicken, and most vegetables; and a more robust sauce for meats, turkey, and duckling. A marinade or sauce should complement, not mask, the flavor of the food. The most important guideline is your own personal preference.

TEXTURE & SIZE: Is the texture soft or firm? Is the food small, medium, or large? These factors help determine the marinating time. For example, foods such as fish fillets require just a brief marinating time, 1 to 2 hours. Because they are small, thin, and porous, fillets will absorb flavor quickly; whereas, large less-tender roasts must marinate for several hours.

TENDERIZING: To tenderize the tougher cuts of meat, a marinade must be made with an acidic liquid, such as vinegar, wine, citrus juices, beer, or ketchup and other tomato-based ingredients. Length of time is also important. Small portions of meat, fish fillets, chicken parts, most vegetables, and similarly sized foods should marinate about 1 to 2 hours. Large cuts of meat should marinate several hours or overnight. Pierce the meat in several places to increase marinade penetration.

SAUCES: Many marinades and basting sauces are interchangeable, or can be used for both purposes. Unless the meat needs tenderizing, the choice to marinate and the length of marinating time are matters of personal preference . . . do you like well-seasoned or milder-flavored foods? The frequency of basting also can be controlled. Start basting at the beginning, midway, or toward the end of grilling, depending on the intensity of flavor desired. If the sauce has a high sugar content, however, limit basting to the last 15 to 20 minutes of grilling in order to prevent burning.

MARINATING: Place the food in a plastic bag, baking dish, or stainless steel, glass, or enameled bowl. Add the marinade; then tightly seal the bag or cover the bowl or dish. Refrigerate for the period indicated in the recipe or determined by preference. Turn the food several times. If desired, the marinade can be drained, strained, and used for basting.

Teriyaki Marinade

Amount: 1 cup

In small bowl, combine ingredients; mix well. Use as marinade or basting sauce for meat, poultry, and seafood.

HOT TERIYAKI SAUCE: Substitute 1 tablespoon grated fresh gingerroot for ground ginger; add 1 clove garlic, minced, and 1/2 teaspoon dry mustard.

- 1/2 cup soy sauce
- 1/4 cup dry sherry
- 2 tablespoons vegetable oil
- 2 tablespoons brown sugar or honey
- 1 teaspoon ground ginger

Barbecue Sauce

Amount: 2 cups

1   small onion, finely chopped
1/4 cup vegetable oil
1   cup ketchup
1/2 cup water
2   tablespoons cider vinegar or
     lemon juice
2   tablespoons honey or brown
     sugar
1   tablespoon paprika
1/2 teaspoon salt
1/4 teaspoon freshly ground
     pepper

For a sweeter sauce, increase honey or sugar to 1/4 cup. Corn syrup may be substituted for honey.

In small saucepan, cook onion in oil until tender; stir in remaining ingredients. Bring to boil; cover. Reduce heat to low; simmer 5 minutes. Use as marinade or basting sauce for meat, poultry, and seafood.

HOT BARBECUE SAUCE: Omit ketchup and paprika; add 1 cup chili sauce and 1 tablespoon chili powder.

MUSTARD BARBECUE SAUCE: Omit vinegar; add 3 tablespoons prepared mustard and 1/8 teaspoon cayenne pepper.

NEW ORLEANS MARINADE: Omit water; add 1/4 cup soy sauce, 1 tablespoon Worchestershire sauce, and 1 teaspoon hot pepper sauce.

Red Wine Marinade

Amount: 1 3/4 cups

1   cup dry red wine
1/4 cup lemon juice
1/4 cup vegetable oil
2   tablespoons sliced green
     onions
1   tablespoon honey or sugar
1   teaspoon basil, crushed
1/4 teaspoon dry mustard
1/4 teaspoon salt
1/4 teaspoon sugar

In small bowl, combine ingredients; mix well. Use as marinade or basting sauce for meat, poultry, and seafood.

WHITE WINE MARINADE: Substitute dry white wine for red wine and 1/2 teaspoon rosemary or thyme, crushed, for basil. Excellent for lamb and seafood!

BEER MARINADE: Substitute 1 cup beer for wine and 1/4 cup soy sauce for lemon juice. Add 1 clove garlic, minced. Best for beef and pork!

LEMON HERB MARINADE: Omit wine and onions; increase lemon juice to 1/2 cup.

Vinaigrette Marinade

Amount: 2 cups

3/4 cup vegetable oil
3/4 cup wine vinegar
1/3 cup soy sauce
2   tablespoons
     Worchestershire sauce
1   tablespoon lemon juice
2   teaspoons sugar
1   teaspoon dry mustard
1   teaspoon salt
1/2 teaspoon freshly ground
     pepper

In small bowl, combine ingredients; mix well. Use as marinade or basting sauce for beef, lamb, chicken, duck, swordfish, tuna, shrimp, and vegetables.

CHILI VINAIGRETTE: Substitute 1/2 cup chili sauce for soy sauce and lemon juice; add 1 teaspoon chili powder or hot pepper sauce.

CURRY MARINADE: Omit vinegar and Worchestershire sauce; add 3/4 cup dry white wine and 1 teaspoon curry powder.

TARRAGON VINAIGRETTE: Omit soy sauce and Worchestershire sauce; add 1 teaspoon tarragon, crushed.

SUPERB SAUCES & MARINADES IN SECONDS

CUMBERLAND SAUCE: In small saucepan, combine $1/2$ cup currant jelly, $1/4$ cup port wine, 2 tablespoons orange juice, and $1/2$ teaspoon grated orange rind; heat thoroughly. Serve with duckling, ham, lamb, pork, or turkey.　　**$3/4$ cup**

DIJON MUSTARD SAUCE: In small bowl, combine $3/4$ cup mayonnaise, 2 tablespoons Dijon mustard, 1 tablespoon chopped green onion or parsley, and $1/8$ teaspoon cayenne pepper; mix well. Chill. Serve with beef, chicken, ham, lamb, or pork.　　**$3/4$ cup**

DILL CREAM SAUCE: In small bowl, combine $3/4$ cup dairy sour cream, $1/2$ cup mayonnaise, 2 tablespoons chopped parsley, $1/2$ teaspoon dill weed, and $1/8$ teaspoon freshly ground pepper; mix well. Chill. Serve with fish, beef, or ham.　　**$1^{1/4}$ cups**

GINGER ORANGE SAUCE: In small saucepan, combine 1 cup orange marmalade, 1 tablespoon lemon juice, 1 tablespoon soy sauce, and 1 teaspoon ground ginger; heat thoroughly. Use as a basting sauce or serve with chicken, duckling, pork, or lamb. Pineapple or apricot preserves can be substituted for marmalade.　　**1 cup**

ITALIAN MARINADE: In small bowl, combine 1 cup Italian dressing, 2 tablespoons very finely chopped onion, and $1/8$ teaspoon oregano, crushed. Use as a marinade or basting sauce for beef, chicken, lamb, and pork.　　**1 cup**

LIME HONEY SAUCE: In small bowl, combine $1/2$ cup dry white wine, $1/4$ cup honey, 2 tablespoons lime or lemon juice, 2 teaspoons chopped mint, and $1/4$ teaspoon coarsely ground pepper; mix well. Use as a marinade and basting sauce or serve with chicken, lamb, or fish.　　**$3/4$ cup**

ORIENTAL SAUCE: In small bowl, combine $2/3$ cup wine vinegar or sherry, $1/2$ cup pineapple juice, $1/4$ cup soy sauce, and 1 teaspoon each dry mustard and grated gingerroot; mix well. Use as a marinade and basting sauce for chicken, duckling, pork, or shrimp.　　**$1^{1/3}$ cups**

HORSERADISH WALNUT SAUCE: In small bowl, combine 1 cup dairy sour cream, 2 to 4 tablespoons prepared horseradish, $1/3$ cup coarsely chopped walnuts, and $1/8$ teaspoon each salt and freshly ground pepper. Chill. Serve with beef, ham, or fish.　　**$1^{1/3}$ cups**

SEASONED BUTTERS

Add one of the following combinations to $1/2$ cup butter or margarine, melted. Use for basting or serve with meats, poultry, seafood, and vegetables.

BLUE CHEESE BUTTER: $1/2$ cup crumbled blue cheese, 1 tablespoon chopped onion, and $1/8$ teaspoon cayenne pepper.

CURRY BUTTER: 2 tablespoons sliced green onions, $1/2$ teaspoon curry powder, and $1/8$ teaspoon freshly ground pepper.

GARLIC CHIVE BUTTER: 2 to 3 garlic cloves, minced; 1 teaspoon chopped chives; and $1/4$ teaspoon lemon-pepper seasoning.

PARSLEY LEMON BUTTER: 2 tablespoons chopped parsley, 1 tablespoon lemon juice, and $1/8$ teaspoon freshly ground pepper.

Steaks, roasts, and burgers . . . any type of beef that can be prepared in a conventional broiler or oven is even more delicious cooked out-of-doors on your gas grill. If beef barbecuing is a new adventure, a few guidelines will point you in the right direction:

AMOUNT: When estimating how much meat to purchase, consider the people that you are serving . . . children, adults, teenagers . . . and judge accordingly. In general, allow the following amounts per person:

Ground Beef	$1/4$ to $1/3$ pound
Steaks and roasts, bone-in	$1/2$ to $3/4$ pound
Steaks and roasts, boneless	$1/3$ to $1/2$ pound

Almost all of the recipes in this chapter can be multiplied or divided to accommodate the number of people to be served.

PREPARATION: Trim excess fat from meat to prevent flare-ups and to eliminate extra calories. If there is a band of fat along the edge of the steak or roast, make slashes at $1^{1}/2$-inch intervals to prevent the meat from curling during grilling. Let meat come to room temperature. To cut raw meat easily, partially freeze it (about 20 minutes) before slicing.

Trim excess fat before grilling.

Slash edge at $1^{1}/2$-inch intervals.

Press peppercorns into steak.

Grilling Time: 14 to 20 minutes

 1   *3- to 4-pound beef top sirloin steak, $1^{1}/2$ inches thick*
 2   *tablespoons vegetable oil*
$1/3$ *cup cracked peppercorns*

SERVES: 4 to 6

Pepper Steak

Trim fat from steak; slash edge at $1^{1}/2$-inch intervals. Brush steak with oil; press peppercorns into both sides of steak.

Remove cooking grids from grill. Preheat grill on high 5 minutes; turn left control to off and right control to medium-low. Return grids to grill; brush right grid with oil.

Place steak on right grid. Close grill top; grill steak 7 to 10 minutes on each side or to desired doneness.

MARINATING: Let small cuts of beef marinate about 1 to 2 hours and large roasts anywhere from 8 to 24 hours, depending on your own flavor preference. For deeper flavor penetration, pierce the meat in many places with a fork or score both sides of less tender steaks and roasts with a knife.

TENDERIZING: Marinades with an acidic base will tenderize beef as well as add flavor. Meat tenderizer also is effective if sprinkled on the meat about 30 minutes before grilling. First be sure to pierce the meat thoroughly .

SEASONING: Beef can be seasoned before or during grilling, or both. Do not salt the meat until it has finished grilling, as salt tends to extract flavorful juices from the meat. Also, once the meat has absorbed flavor from the other herbs and spices, you may find that salting is unnecessary.

BARBECUE SAUCES: In addition to the many marinades and sauces featured in this book, there is a vast variety of prepared sauces available in supermarkets and speciality stores. Also, pourable dressings are excellent marinades and basting sauces. Try Italian, oil and vinegar, red wine vinegar and oil, French, Russian, or combinations of these dressings. Be creative!

GRILLING: If you wish to sear the meat, place it on the grids or rotisserie after preheating the grill. Close the grill top and grill on high for 1 to 3 minutes or until browned. Then open the top and cool the grill to the desired grilling temperature. Most cuts of beef should be grilled at medium to low temperatures. Use a spatula or tongs, not a fork, to turn meat during grilling, since piercing the meat will allow natural juices to escape. Test steaks for doneness by making a small slit near the bone or in thickest part of the steak. Check roasts with a meat thermometer. For even browning and cooking, grill large roasts on the rotisserie. Large cuts of meat continue to cook after they have been removed from the grill. To avoid overcooking, remove meat from the grill when the internal temperature reaches 5 to 10 degrees below the desired serving temperature.

Steak & Mushrooms

Grilling Time: 16 to 20 minutes

Trim fat from steak; slash edge at 1½-inch intervals. Place in baking dish. In small bowl, combine onion, wine, oil, lemon juice, Worchestershire, garlic, salt, and pepper; mix well. Pour marinade over steak. Cover; refrigerate 2 hours, turning occasionally.

Remove cooking grids from grill. Preheat grill on high 5 minutes; turn left control to off and right control to medium. Return grids to grill; brush right grill with oil.

Drain steak, reserving marinade; place on right grid. Close grill top; grill steak 8 to 10 minutes on each side or to desired doneness, occasionally brushing with marinade. Sauté mushrooms in butter until tender; serve with steak.

1	1 ½-pound beef top sirloin steak, 1 inch thick
½	cup finely chopped onion
½	cup dry red wine
¼	cup vegetable oil
2	tablespoons lemon juice
1	teaspoon Worchestershire sauce
1	clove garlic, minced
½	teaspoon salt
¼	teaspoon freshly ground pepper
1	pound fresh mushrooms
⅓	cup butter or margarine

SERVES: 4 to 6

BEEF GRILLING TIMETABLE

CUT	SIZE/ WEIGHT	DONENESS/ TEMPERATURE	GRILL SETTING	TOTAL TIME*
Brisket	3 pounds	Rare (140° F.)	Low	2 - 2 ½ hours
		Medium (160° F.)	Low	2 ½ - 3 hours
		Well (170° F.)	Low	3 - 3 ½ hours
	5 pounds	Rare (140° F.)	Low	3 - 4 ½ hours
		Medium (160° F.)	Low	4 ½ - 5 hours
		Well (170° F.)	Low	5 - 5 ½ hours
Hamburgers	¼ pound (½ inch thick)	Rare	Medium	8 - 9 minutes
		Medium	Medium	10 - 11 minutes
		Well Done	Medium	12 - 14 minutes
Kabobs	1 ½ inch cubes	Rare	Medium	5 minutes
		Medium	Medium	8 minutes
		Well Done	Medium	10 minutes
Roasts				
Rib (rolled) (rotisserie)	5 pounds	Rare (140° F.)	Low	1 ½ - 2 ½ hours
		Medium (160° F.)	Low	2 - 3 hours
		Well Done (170° F.)	Low	3 - 3 ½ hours
Rib (standing)	5 pounds	Rare (140° F.)	Low	1 ½ - 2 hours
		Medium (160° F.)	Low	2 - 3 hours
		Well Done (170° F.)	Low	2 - 3 hours
Rump, Tip, Top Round	3 pounds	Rare (140° F.)	Low	50 - 60 minutes
		Medium (160° F.)	Low	1 - 1 ½ hours
		Well done (170° F.)	Low	1 ½ - 2 hours
	5 pounds	Rare (140° F.)	Low	1 - 1 ½ hours
		Medium (160° F.)	Low	1 ½ - 2 hours
		Well Done (170° F.)	Low	2 - 2 ½ hours
Tenderloin	2 - 3 pounds	Rare (140° F.)	Medium	25 - 30 minutes
	4 - 6 pounds	Rare (140° F.)	Medium	35 - 40 minutes
Steaks				
Chuck	1 inch thick	Rare	Med. High	20 - 25 minutes
		Medium	Med. High	25 - 40 minutes
		Well Done	Med. High	30 - 35 minutes
Flank	1 inch thick	Rare	Medium	10 - 14 minutes
		Medium	Medium	15 - 20 minutes
Rib, Boneless Top Loin, Porterhouse, Sirloin, T-Bone, Top Round	1 inch thick	Rare	Med. Low	5 - 6 minutes
		Medium	Med. Low	6 - 8 minutes
		Well Done	Med. Low	8 - 10 minutes
	1 ½ inches thick	Rare	Med. Low	10 - 15 minutes
		Medium	Med. Low	15 - 20 minutes
		Well Done	Med. Low	20 - 25 minutes
	2 inches thick	Rare	Med. Low	14 - 20 minutes
		Medium	Med. Low	20 - 25 minutes
		Well Done	Med. Low	25 - 30 minutes
Tenderloin, Filet Mignon	¼ - ½ pound	Rare	Medium	3 - 5 minutes
		Medium	Medium	5 - 8 minutes

* Approximate grilling time is based on grilling with the grill top closed.

Steak a la Grenadier

Grilling Time: 16 to 20 minutes

Trim fat from steak; slash edge at 1 1/2-inch intervals. Place in baking dish.

In medium saucepan, sauté mushrooms and onions in butter 5 minutes or until onions are crisp-tender; cool. Add wine, Worchestershire, and brown sauce. Pour over steak. Cover; refrigerate 4 hours, turning occasionally.

Remove cooking grids from grill. Preheat grill on high 5 minutes; turn left control to off and right control to medium. Return grids to grill; brush right grid with oil.

Drain steak, reserving mushroom mixture; place steak on right grid. Close grill top; grill steak 8 to 10 minutes on each side or to desired doneness.

Return mushroom mixture to saucepan. Add mushroom soup and heat thoroughly, whisking to smooth sauce. Serve over steak.

1	1 1/2-pound beef top sirloin steak, 1 inch thick
1	cup sliced fresh medium mushrooms
1/2	cup chopped green onions
4	tablespoons butter or margarine
1/2	cup Madeira wine
2	teaspoons Worchestershire sauce
2	teaspoons bottled brown sauce
1	10 3/4-ounce can golden mushroom soup, undiluted

SERVES: 4 to 6

Marinated Flank Steak

Grilling Time: 20 to 24 minutes

Place steak in baking dish. In small bowl, combine wine, chopped onion, marjoram, thyme, and bay leaf; mix well. Pour marinade over steak. Cover; refrigerate 4 hours, turning occasionally.

Remove cooking grids from grill. Preheat grill on high 5 minutes; turn controls to medium. Return grids to grill; brush with oil.

Brush onion slices with butter; sprinkle with lemon pepper. Drain steak, reserving marinade. Discard bay leaf. Arrange steak and onions on grids. Close grill top; grill steak and onions 10 to 12 minutes on each side or to desired doneness, occasionally brushing with marinade. Place steak on cutting board; with knife slanted, carve steak across the grain into thin slices. Serve with onions.

1	1 1/2-pound beef flank steak, 1 inch thick
1/3	cup red wine
1/4	cup finely chopped onion
1/4	teaspoon marjoram, crushed
1/4	teaspoon thyme, crushed
1	bay leaf
3	medium onions, cut into 1/2-inch slices
1/4	cup butter or margarine, melted
	Lemon-pepper seasoning

SERVES: 4 to 6

London Grill

Grilling Time: 10 to 14 minutes

Score steak on both sides in 1-inch diamond pattern. In small bowl, combine remaining ingredients; mix well. Brush sauce on steak, reserving remainder.

Remove cooking grids from grill. Preheat grill on high 5 minutes; turn left control to off and right control to medium. Return grids to grill; brush with oil.

Place steak on right grid. Close grill top; grill steak 5 to 7 minutes on each side, frequently brushing with sauce. Place steak on cutting board; with knife slanted, carve steak across the grain into thin slices.

1	1 1/2-pound beef flank steak, 2 inches thick
1/4	cup vegetable oil
1	tablespoon lemon juice
1	tablespoon finely chopped parsley
1	clove garlic, minced
1/4	teaspoon coarsely ground pepper
1/4	teaspoon salt

SERVES: 4 to 6

1/4   cup butter or margarine,
         melted
2   tablespoons
         Worchestershire sauce
2   tablespoons lemon juice
1   tablespoon finely chopped
         parsley
1/2   teaspoon freshly ground
         pepper
1/2   teaspoon thyme or
         rosemary, crushed
1/8   teaspoon cayenne pepper
6   1/2-pound beef cubed steaks

SERVES: 6

Garlic Steaks

In small bowl, combine all ingredients, except steaks; mix well.

Remove cooking grids from grill. Preheat grill on high 5 minutes. Return grids to grill; brush with oil.

Brush steaks with sauce; place directly on grids or in Broiler Basket on grids. Close grill top; grill steaks 2 to 3 minutes on each side or to desired doneness. Brush steaks with remaining sauce before serving.

STEAK SANDWICHES: Split 6 large rolls; spread with butter or margarine. Place on grids, cut side down, to toast. Serve steaks in rolls with grilled green pepper and onion slices.

1   3-pound beef porterhouse or
         top sirloin steak, 1 1/2
         inches thick
      Garlic powder
      Freshly ground pepper

SERVES: 6

Boneless top loin or T-bone steaks (10 to 14 ounces each) can be substituted for a larger steak. Arrange 2 inches apart on grids; grill 5 to 8 minutes on each side or to desired doneness.

Grilled Steak

Trim fat from steak; slash edge at 1 1/2-inch intervals. Sprinkle steak with garlic powder and pepper.

Remove cooking grids from grill. Preheat grill on high 5 minutes; turn controls to medium-low. Return grids to grill; brush with oil.

Place steaks on grids. Close grill top; grill 7 to 10 minutes on each side or to desired doneness.

ITALIAN BEEF STEAK: Substitute Italian seasonings for garlic powder; brush steak with olive oil before seasoning.

Grilled Steak→

ALL THE BEST BURGERS

Grilled Beef Burgers

In large bowl, combine meat and seasonings; mix lightly. Shape into 6 oval or round patties, ¹/₂ inch thick. Spread cut side of buns with butter.

Remove grids from grill. Preheat grill on high 5 minutes; turn controls to medium. Return grids to grill; brush with oil.

Place beef patties on grids. Close grill top; grill patties 4 to 6 minutes on each side or to desired doneness. During last 5 minutes, place buns, cut side down, around edge of grids. Serve beef burgers in buns with selection of condiments.

Grilling Time: 8 to 12 minutes

1¹/₂	pounds lean ground beef
¹/₄	teaspoon salt
¹/₄	teaspoon freshly ground pepper
6	hamburger buns, split
¹/₄	cup butter or margarine

SERVES: 6

A GRILLED BURGER
SPEAKS FOR ITSELF!

ALL AMERICAN BURGERS: Serve burgers in grilled sesame buns with processed American cheese slices, thinly sliced onions and tomatoes, ketchup, and mustard.

BACON BURGERS: Serve burgers between grilled Vienna bread slices with crisply cooked bacon strips, tomato slices, and salad dressing.

BARBECUED BURGERS: Add $^1/_4$ cup bottled barbecue sauce to meat mixture. During grilling, brush patties with additional barbecue sauce. Serve in heated sesame buns with grilled onions.

BLUE CHEESE BURGERS: During last 3 minutes of grilling, top each burger with 1 to 2 tablespoons of crumbled blue or Roquefort cheese. Serve in heated Kaiser rolls with sliced mushrooms and green onions.

MUFFIN BURGERS: During last 3 minutes of grilling, top burgers with slices of Cheddar cheese and tomato. Serve in toasted and buttered English muffins.

CALIFORNIA BURGERS: Omit salt; add 2 tablespoons soy sauce to meat mixture. Serve burgers between slices of coarse whole-wheat bread with alfalfa sprouts and thinly sliced avocados, cucumbers, and tomatoes.

BAVARIAN BURGERS: During last 3 minutes of grilling, top burgers with slices of Muenster cheese. Serve between grilled rye bread slices with horseradish mustard and dill pickle slices.

DOUBLE BURGERS: Shape meat mixture into 12 thin patties; grill 3 to 4 minutes on each side. Top each patty with slice each of cheese, onion, and green pepper. Fill each poppy seed bun with 2 patties, ketchup, and mustard.

GRILLED GREEK BURGERS: Serve burgers in heated pita bread with sautéed onions and green pepper, thinly sliced tomato, and crumbled feta cheese.

MEXI-BURGERS: Add 1 teaspoon chili powder and $^1/_4$ teaspoon oregano, crushed, to meat mixture. Serve burgers on heated flour tortillas with chopped lettuce, sliced avocado, chopped red and yellow pepper, shredded Cheddar cheese, and taco sauce. Top with dairy sour cream and guacamole, if desired.

Grilled Greek Burgers

MUSHROOM BURGERS: Sauté $1^1/_2$ cups sliced mushrooms and $^1/_2$ cup chopped onion in small amount of Italian dressing. Serve burgers between slices of Vienna bread with mushrooms and onions.

OLIVE BURGERS: Shape meat mixture into 12 patties; top 6 patties with 1 tablespoon chopped stuffed olives. Cover with remaining patties; press edges to seal. During grilling, brush patties with Italian dressing. Serve in hamburger buns with shredded mozzarella cheese.

PIZZA BURGERS: Add $^1/_4$ cup pizza sauce and $^1/_4$ cup finely chopped onion to meat mixture. During grilling, brush patties with additional pizza sauce. Serve in heated pita bread with chopped green pepper and shredded mozzarella cheese.

REUBEN BURGERS: Serve burgers between grilled rye bread slices, or in rye hamburger buns with heated sauerkraut, slices of Swiss cheese, and thousand island dressing.

Mexi-Burgers

2 *pounds veal cutlets*
1/3 *cup vegetable oil*
1/4 *cup lemon juice*
2 *tablespoons chopped parsley*
1 *tablespoon sliced green onion*
1 *clove garlic, minced (optional)*
1/2 *teaspoon salt*
1/8 *teaspoon cayenne pepper*

SERVES: 6

To facilitate turning, the cutlets can be grilled in a Thermos® Broiler Basket or Hamburger Broiler that has been brushed with oil.

Grilled Veal Picata

With meat mallet or dull side of French knife blade, pound cutlets to 1/4-inch thickness. Place cutlets in baking dish. In small bowl, combine remaining ingredients; mix well. Pour marinade over cutlets. Cover; refrigerate 2 hours, turning occasionally.

Remove cooking grids from grill. Preheat grill on high 5 minutes; turn left control to off and right control to low. Return grids to grill; brush with oil.

Drain cutlets, reserving marinade; arrange cutlets on right grid. Close grill top; grill cutlets 4 to 5 minutes on each side, occasionally brushing with marinade.

---

1 *4-pound beef brisket*
1 *cup dry red wine*
1 *cup ketchup*
2 *tablespoons brown sugar*
2 *tablespoons cider vinegar*
1 *tablespoon prepared horseradish*
1 *tablespoon prepared mustard*
1 *tablespoon instant minced onion*
1/2 *teaspoon salt*
1/4 *teaspoon freshly ground pepper*

SERVES: 6 to 8

Barbecued Brisket

Place meat in baking dish. In small bowl, combine remaining ingredients; mix well. Pour marinade over meat. Cover; refrigerate 8 hours, turning occasionally.

Remove grids from grill. Preheat grill on high 5 minutes; turn right control to off and left control to low. Return grids to grill; brush right grid with oil.

Drain meat, reserving marinade; place meat on right grid. Close grill top; grill meat 2½ hours or to desired doneness, occasionally brushing with marinade. Place meat on cutting board; with knife slanted, carve meat across grain into thin slices.

HOT & SPICY BRISKET: Substitute Hot Barbecue Sauce (page 14) for marinade. Increase water in sauce to 2/3 cup. During last 30 minutes, top with sliced green pepper and onion.

Marinating for several hours will add extra flavor to Barbecued Brisket.

To ensure tender meat, brisket must be cut across the grain with knife slanted.

Fajitas

Score steak on both sides in 1-inch diamond pattern; place in baking dish. In small bowl, combine 1/3 cup oil, lime juice, garlic, chili powder, oregano, salt, and cayenne; mix well. Pour marinade over steak. Cover; refrigerate 12 hours, turning occasionally.

Remove cooking grids from grill. Preheat grill on high 5 minutes; turn left control to low and right control to medium. Return grids to grill; brush right grid with oil.

In large skillet or wok, stir-fry onions and peppers in remaining oil with black pepper until crisp-tender. Place skillet on left grid to stay hot. Wrap stack of tortillas in foil; heat on left grid, turning occasionally.

Drain steak, reserving marinade; place on right grid. Close grill top; grill steak 10 to 12 minutes on each side or to desired doneness, occasionally brushing with marinade. Place steak on cutting board; with knife slanted, carve steak across the grain into thin slices. Serve in tortillas with onions and peppers, cheese, guacamole, salsa, and sour cream.

1	1 1/2-pound beef flank steak, 1 inch thick
1/2	cup vegetable oil, divided
1/3	cup lime or lemon juice
2	cloves garlic, minced
2	teaspoons chili powder
1/2	teaspoon oregano, crushed
1/4	teaspoon salt
1/8	teaspoon cayenne pepper
2	medium onions, thinly sliced
2	green peppers, cut into strips
1/4	teaspoon freshly ground black pepper
10	flour tortillas
2	cups (8 ounces) shredded Cheddar cheese
	Guacamole
	Salsa
	Dairy sour cream

SERVES: 5 to 6

Sukiyaki

In small bowl, combine sherry, soy sauce, and cornstarch; mix well. Stir in ginger, salt, and pepper.

Remove cooking grids from grill. Preheat grill on high 5 minutes. Return grids to grill.

Place large iron skillet on grids. Close grill top; heat skillet 20 to 25 minutes. Add oil; heat until very hot. Add meat and onions; stir-fry until meat is browned on all sides.

Stir in bean sprouts, water chestnuts, snow peas, and tomatoes. Close grill top; cook 2 to 3 minutes or until thoroughly heated. Add sherry sauce to meat-vegetable mixture; cook, stirring constantly, until sauce is clear and thickened. Serve with rice.

1/4	cup dry sherry or water
2	tablespoons soy sauce
1	teaspoon cornstarch
1	tablespoon grated fresh gingerroot
1/2	teaspoon salt
1/4	teaspoon freshly ground pepper
2	tablespoons vegetable oil
1 1/2	pounds beef top round or sirloin steak, cut into thin slices
3/4	cup sliced green onions
1	cup fresh bean sprouts
1	8-ounce can sliced water chestnuts, drained
1	6-ounce package frozen snow peas
8	cherry tomatoes, halved
4	cups hot cooked rice

SERVES: 6

1 4-to 6-pound beef tip, boneless
    prime rib, rib eye, or
    boneless rump roast
³/₄ cup dry red wine
¹/₂ cup ketchup
¹/₂ cup vegetable oil
¹/₄ cup finely chopped onion
1 teaspoon rosemary, crushed
¹/₂ teaspoon salt
¹/₄ teaspoon coarsely ground
    pepper

SERVES: 6 to 10

Meat is seared quickly on high heat to brown the surface and to seal in juices.

Roast Beef on a Spit

Trim fat from roast; place in baking dish. In small bowl, combine remaining ingredients; mix well. Pour marinade over roast. Cover; refrigerate 8 hours, turning occasionally.

Remove cooking grids from grill. Place drip pan on lava rocks in center of grill. Preheat grill on high 5 minutes.

Drain roast, reserving marinade. Insert spit rod lengthwise through roast. Secure holding forks; check balance. Attach to rotisserie; start motor. Close grill top; spit-roast on high 5 minutes or until roast is seared. Turn controls to low; spit-roast 1¹/₂ to 3 hours or to desired doneness, occasionally brushing roast with marinade.

BEEF ROAST CARBONADE: Substitute Beer Marinade (page 14) for marinade.

BEEF ROAST VINAIGRETTE: Substitute Vinaigrette Marinade (page 14) for marinade. Grill roast directly on the grids, occasionally turning and brushing with marinade.

1 3-pound beef tenderloin roast
¹/₂ cup dry red wine
¹/₂ cup soy sauce
2 tablespoons vegetable oil
3 cloves garlic, minced
1 teaspoon hot pepper sauce
¹/₄ teaspoon freshly ground
    pepper

SERVES: 6

Tenderloin Au Vin

Place meat in baking dish. In small bowl, combine remaining ingredients; mix well. Pour marinade over meat. Cover; refrigerate 24 hours, turning occasionally.

Remove cooking grids from grill. Preheat grill on high 5 minutes; turn left control to off and right control to medium. Return grids to grill; brush right grid with oil.

Drain meat, reserving marinade; place on right grid. Close grill top; grill meat 25 minutes or to desired doneness, occasionally brushing with marinade. Let stand 10 minutes before carving.

Sesame Roast Beef

Rub surface of roast with butter. With fork, pierce roast in many places; sprinkle with tenderizer. Place in baking dish. In small bowl, combine remaining ingredients; mix well. Pour marinade over roast. Cover; refrigerate 3 hours, turning occasionally.

Remove cooking grids from grill; place drip pan on lava rocks on right side of grill. Preheat grill on high 5 minutes; turn left control to off and right control to medium high. Return grids to grill; brush right grid with oil.

Drain roast, reserving marinade; place on right grid. Close grill top; grill roast 1 to 1½ hours or to desired doneness, occasionally turning and brushing with marinade. Place roast on cutting board; with knife slanted, carve roast across the grain into thin slices.

1   3-pound beef boneless shoulder pot or blade roast, 1 inch thick
    Butter or margarine
    Instant meat tenderizer
1   large onion, finely chopped
½   cup strong coffee
½   cup soy sauce
1   tablespoon cider vinegar
1   tablespoon sesame seed, toasted
¼   teaspoon basil, crushed

SERVES: 6 to 8

Grilled Rosemary Roast

Place roast in baking dish. In small skillet, sauté garlic in oil 2 to 3 minutes; remove from heat. Stir in remaining ingredients; pour marinade over roast. Cover; refrigerate 8 hours, turning occasionally.

Remove grids from grill. Preheat grill on high 5 minutes; turn left control to off and right control to low. Return grids to grill; brush right grid with oil.

Drain roast, reserving marinade; place on right grid. Close grill top; grill roast 1 to 1½ hours or to desired doneness, frequently turning and brushing with marinade. Place roast on cutting board; with knife slanted, carve roast across the grain into thin slices.

SAVORY ROAST: Omit soy sauce and sugar; increase wine vinegar to ¼ cup. Add ¼ teaspoon ground savory.

1   3-pound beef boneless shoulder pot or blade roast, 1 inch thick
2   cloves garlic, minced
2   tablespoons vegetable oil
2   tablespoons brown sugar or corn syrup
2   tablespoons lemon juice
2   tablespoons red or white wine vinegar
1   tablespoon soy sauce
¼   teaspoon dry mustard
¼   teaspoon rosemary, crushed
¼   teaspoon Worchestershire sauce

SERVES: 6 to 8

Beef and Vegetable Kabobs

2 *pounds beef top round steak,*
   cut into 1¹/₂-inch cubes
1 *cup dry red wine*
¹/₃ *cup soy sauce*
¹/₃ *cup vegetable oil*
1 *clove garlic, minced*
¹/₂ *teaspoon oregano, crushed*
¹/₈ *teaspoon freshly ground*
   pepper
12 *large mushroom caps*
2 *green peppers, cut into*
   1¹/₂-inch squares
2 *red peppers, cut into 1¹/₂-inch*
   squares

SERVES: 4 to 6

Place meat in baking dish. In small bowl, combine wine, soy sauce, oil, garlic, oregano, and ground pepper; mix well. Pour marinade over meat. Cover; refrigerate 2 hours, turning occasionally.

Remove cooking grids from grill. Preheat grill on high 5 minutes; turn left control to off and right control to medium. Return grids to grill; brush right grid with oil.

Drain meat, reserving marinade. Thread meat on long metal skewers. Alternately thread mushrooms and peppers on long skewers. Arrange meat kabobs on right grid; brush with marinade. Close grill top; grill meat kabobs 18 to 22 minutes, frequently turning and brushing with marinade. During last 10 minutes, grill vegetable kabobs, occasionally turning and brushing with marinade.

A Thermos® Kabob Set with 12-inch skewers and a raised rack is ideal for grilling kabobs.

Curried Beef Kabobs

3 *pounds beef top round or*
   sirloin steak, cut into
   1¹/₂-inch cubes
¹/₂ *cup vegetable oil*
¹/₄ *cup lemon juice*
2 *cloves garlic, minced*
   (optional)
1 *to 2 tablespoons curry powder*
1 *tablespoon sugar*
¹/₄ *teaspoon salt*
   Hot cooked brown or white rice

SERVES: 6 to 8

Place meat in baking dish. In small bowl, combine remaining ingredients, except rice; mix well. Pour marinade over meat; turn lightly to coat. Cover; refrigerate 2 hours, turning occasionally.

Remove cooking grids from grill. Preheat grill on high 5 minutes; turn left control to off and right control to medium. Return grids to grill; brush right grid with oil.

Drain meat, reserving marinade. Thread meat on long metal skewers. Arrange kabobs on right grid; brush with marinade. Close grill top; grill kabobs 18 to 22 minutes, frequently turning and brushing with marinade. Remove meat from skewers; serve on rice.

A Thermos® Kabob Set with 12-inch skewers and a raised rack is ideal for grilling kabobs.

Crown Roast on the Grill (page 39) →

GREAT GRILLED PORK

What is more enticing than the wonderful aroma of pork barbecuing on the grill! Pork adapts to outdoor grilling with the greatest of ease and pleasure. The recipes and information in this chapter focus on chops, steaks, roasts, and hams; ribs and sausages are featured in the next chapters. Before you start grilling with pork, a few "nice to know" facts may be of help:

STORAGE: Pork is available in fresh, cured, smoked, and canned forms. Fresh pork can be stored in the refrigerator for 2 to 3 days, wrapped loosely in waxed paper or foil. Cured or smoked pork is usually prepackaged and can be refrigerated in the original wrap for 1 to 2 weeks.

AMOUNT: To estimate the amount of meat to purchase per serving, follow these general guidelines:

Chops and steaks	$1/3$ to $1/2$ pound
Cutlets	$1/4$ to $1/3$ pound
Ground pork	$1/4$ pound
Roasts, bone-in	$1/3$ to $1/2$ pound
Roasts, boneless	$1/4$ to $1/2$ pound

Most of the recipes in this chapter can be multiplied or divided to accommodate the number of people to be served.

PREPARATION: Pork requires almost no advance preparation. However, if you are planning something special, like grilling a crown roast or planning a rib feast for fifty, alert the butcher in advance. As with all meat, remember the basics: rinse and pat dry with paper towels, then trim excess fat to prevent spattering and flare-ups. Score the fat on large hams.

MARINADES & SAUCES: As pork is already a tender meat, a marinade is only used for added flavor. Many of the recipes in the chapter "Basting Sauces, Marinades, & More" (pages 13-15) are compatible with pork. Teriyaki Marinade (page 13) and Curry Marinade (page 14) are special favorites. Sweet fruit glazes brushed on the meat toward the end of grilling are particularly delicious with ham.

GRILLING: Because all cuts of fresh pork should be thoroughly cooked, you will notice that there are no times indicated for "rare" or "medium" on the Pork Grilling Timetable. Cured pork, most commonly known as "ham," can be purchased as fully cooked or cook-before-eating. Since fully cooked hams, the most prevalent type, are ready to eat as purchased, grilling is primarily for heating and glazing. The cook-before-eating variety must be cooked as well as heated. Check the label or consult your butcher to be sure you know which type you are grilling. To reduce flare-ups, a drip pan should be placed on the lava rocks when grilling large cuts of pork or those with a considerable amount of fat marbling. The leaner boneless hams do not need a drip pan.

Barbecued Pork Chops

Trim fat from chops; slash edge at 1-inch intervals. In small bowl, combine butter and basil; mix well. Remove pulp from zucchini, leaving ¼-inch shell. Chop pulp; refill zucchini. Sprinkle with pepper and cheese.

Remove cooking grids from grill. Preheat grill on high 5 minutes; turn controls to low. Return grids to grill; brush with oil.

Brush chops with barbecue sauce. Arrange chops and zucchini on grids. Close grill top; grill chops and zucchini 8 to 10 minutes or until done, occasionally brushing chops with sauce.

JIFFY BARBECUED CHOPS: Combine 1 cup of your favorite barbecue sauce and ¼ cup finely chopped onion; substitute for Barbecue Sauce.

Grilling Time: 16 to 20 minutes

6   pork loin butterfly chops, ½ inch thick
¼   cup butter or margarine, melted
¼   teaspoon basil or rosemary, crushed
     Barbecue Sauce (page 14)
6   small zucchini, halved lengthwise
     Freshly ground pepper
¾   cup (3 ounces) shredded Cheddar cheese

SERVES: 6

Grilled Pork Burgers

Barbecued Pork Chops with Stuffed Zucchini

Grilled Pork Burgers

In large bowl, combine meat, crumbs, soy sauce, rosemary, sage, and pepper; mix lightly.

Remove cooking grids from grill; place drip pan on lava rocks in center of grill. Preheat grill on high 5 minutes; turn controls to medium-low. Return grids to grill; brush with oil.

Shape meat mixture into 6 patties, ½ inch thick; arrange on grids over drip pan. Close grill top; grill patties 6 to 8 minutes on each side or until done. During last 8 minutes, arrange onion slices and bread around edge of grids. Serve patties between grilled bread slices with onions and cheese.

BARBECUED PORK BURGERS: Add ¼ cup finely chopped onion to meat mixture. Brush patties with your favorite barbecue sauce during grilling.

Grilling Time: 12 to 16 minutes

1½   pounds ground pork
¼   cup dry bread crumbs
2   tablespoons soy sauce
½   teaspoon rosemary, crushed
½   teaspoon ground sage
¼   teaspoon freshly ground pepper
2   large onions, cut into ¼-inch slices
12   slices rye bread
6   slices mozzarella cheese (optional)

SERVES: 6

Stuffed Pork Chops

Trim fat from chops. Cut pocket in each chop from fat edge almost to bone. Sauté apples, raisins, and curry powder in butter until fruit is tender. Stir in 2 tablespoons sherry. Spoon mixture into pockets, fasten with toothpicks. Sprinkle chops with pepper.

Remove grids from grill. Preheat grill on high 5 minutes; turn controls to low. Return grids to grill; brush with oil.

Arrange chops on grids; brush with sherry. Close grill top; grill chops 12 to 15 minutes on each side or until done, occasionally brushing with sherry.

CUMBERLAND CHOPS: Substitute port wine for sherry. Serve with Cumberland Sauce (page 15).

Grilling Time: 24 to 30 minutes

4   pork rib chops, 1¼ inches thick
1   large apple, peeled, cored, and chopped
¼   cup raisins
⅛   teaspoon curry powder
1   tablespoon butter or margarine
    Dry sherry
    Freshly ground pepper

SERVES: 4

SPICY PINEAPPLE CHOPS: Substitute 1 cup crushed pineapple, drained, for apples and ¼ teaspoon mace or nutmeg for curry powder.

Grilled Pork Chops

Trim fat from chops; slash edge at 1-inch intervals. In small bowl, combine remaining ingredients; mix well. Sprinkle seasoning mixture on both sides of chops.

Remove cooking grids from grill. Preheat grill on high 5 minutes; turn controls to low. Return grids to grill; brush with oil.

Arrange chops on grids. Close grill top; grill chops 12 to 15 minutes on each side or until done.

Grilling Time: 24 to 30 minutes

4   pork loin or rib chops, 1 inch thick
1   teaspoon lemon-pepper seasoning
½   teaspoon oregano, crushed
½   teaspoon cayenne pepper

SERVES: 4

Glazed Pork Chops

Trim fat from chops; slash edge at 1-inch intervals. In small bowl, combine remaining ingredients; mix well.

Remove cooking grids from grill. Preheat grill on high 5 minutes; turn controls to low. Return grids to grill; brush with oil.

Arrange chops on grids. Close grill top; grill chops 12 to 15 minutes on each side or until done. During last 10 minutes, frequently brush with glaze.

PINEAPPLE GLAZED CHOPS: Substitute pineapple preserves for apricot preserves and dry white wine for soy sauce.

Grilling Time: 24 to 30 minutes

4   pork loin or rib chops, 1 inch thick
¼   cup apricot preserves or orange marmalade
2   tablespoons soy sauce
1   teaspoon ground ginger
¼   teaspoon freshly ground pepper

SERVES: 4

One tablespoon grated gingerroot can be substituted for ground ginger.

← **Glazed Pork Chop**

PORK GRILLING TIMETABLE

CUT	SIZE/WEIGHT	GRILL SETTING	TOTAL TIME*
Fresh			
Chops, loin or rib	½ inch thick	Low	15 - 20 minutes
	1 inch thick	Low	25 - 30 minutes
Kabobs	1½-inch cubes	Low	15 - 20 minutes
Roast, bone-in	3 - 5 pounds	Low	1½ - 3½ hours (170° F.)
	5 - 8 pounds	Low	2½ - 4½ hours (170° F.)
Roast, boneless	3 - 4 pounds	Low	1½ - 2 hours (170° F.)
	5 - 8 pounds	Low	2½ - 4 hours (170° F.)
Steaks	½ inch thick	Low	15 - 20 minutes
Cured			
Ham Slice	½ inch thick	Low	12 - 15 minutes
	1 inch thick	Low	20 - 24 minutes
Ham, bone-in, fully-cooked	3 - 5 pounds	Low	1 - 2 hours (140° F.)
	7 - 8 pounds	Low	2 - 3½ hours (130° - 140° F.)
Ham, boneless, fully-cooked	3 - 4 pounds	Low	1 - 2 hours (130° - 140° F.)
	4 - 6 pounds	Low	1¼ - 2½ hours (130° - 140° F.)
	8 - 12 pounds	Low	2 - 3½ hours (130° - 140° F.)
Ham, bone in, cook-before-eating	3 - 5 pounds	Low	1¾ - 3¼ hours (170° F.)
	7 - 8 pounds	Low	2½ - 3½ hours (170° F.)
Ham, boneless, cook-before-eating	5 - 8 pounds	Low	2 - 2½ hours (170° F.)
Spareribs	4 pounds	Low	1 - 1¼ hours
Country-Style Ribs	4 pounds	Low	45 - 60 minutes
Bacon	4 slices	High (on griddle)	5 - 8 minutes
Canadian Bacon	6 - 8 slices ¼ inch thick	High (on griddle)	3 minutes
	6 - 8 slices ½ inch thick	High (on griddle)	5 minutes

* Approximate grilling time is based on grilling with the grill top closed.

Curried Pork Cutlets

Grilling Time: 10 to 12 minutes

Trim fat from cutlets; place in baking dish. In small bowl, combine remaining ingredients; mix well. Pour marinade over cutlets. Cover; refrigerate $1/2$ hour, turning once.

Remove cooking grids from grill. Preheat grill on high 5 minutes; turn controls to medium-low. Return grids to grill; brush with oil.

Drain cutlets, reserving marinade; arrange cutlets on grids. Close grill top; grill cutlets 5 to 6 minutes on each side or until done, frequently brushing with marinade.

6   pork sirloin cutlets, $1/4$ inch thick
$1/2$ cup dry white wine or apple juice
1   tablespoon chopped green onion or parsley
1   tablespoon soy sauce
1   tablespoon vegetable oil
2   teaspoons curry powder
$1/4$ teaspoon salt
$1/8$ teaspoon sugar

SERVES: 4 to 6

Chili Chops

Grilling Time: 20 to 24 minutes

Trim fat from chops; place in baking dish. In small bowl, combine remaining ingredients, except green pepper; mix well. Pour marinade over chops. Cover; refrigerate 2 hours, turning once.

Remove cooking grids from grill. Preheat grill on high 5 minutes; turn controls to low. Return grids to grill; brush with oil.

Drain chops, reserving marinade; arrange chops on grids. Close grill top; grill chops 10 to 12 minutes on each side or until done, occasionally brushing with marinade. During last 5 minutes, top with green peppers.

HOT CHOPS: Increase chili powder to 2 tablespoons. Substitute $1/4$ cup dry red wine for water. Add 1 clove garlic, minced, and a few drops hot pepper sauce.

6   pork loin or rib chops, $3/4$ inch thick
$1/2$ cup chili sauce
2   tablespoons vegetable oil
2   tablespoons water
1   tablespoon chili powder
$1/2$ teaspoon dry mustard
$1/4$ teaspoon salt
1   medium green pepper, cut into thin rings

SERVES: 6

Pork Steaks Vinaigrette

Grilling Time: 16 to 20 minutes

Trim fat from steaks; place in baking dish. Pour marinade over steaks. Cover; refrigerate 1 hour, turning once.

Remove cooking grids from grill. Preheat grill on high 5 minutes; turn controls to low. Return grids to grill; brush with oil.

Drain steaks, reserving marinade; arrange steaks on grids. Close grill top; grill steaks 8 to 10 minutes on each side or until done, occasionally brushing with marinade.

4   pork blade steaks, $1/2$ inch thick
1   cup Tarragon Vinaigrette (page 14)

SERVES: 4

Unused marinades and sauces can be refrigerated for future marinating and grilling. Do not keep marinade or sauce that has been in contact with the meat.

Grilled Pork Steaks

Grilling Time: 16 to 20 minutes

4	pork blade steaks, $1/2$ inch thick
$1/3$	cup dry red wine or red wine vinegar
2	tablespoons soy sauce
1	tablespoon vegetable oil
$1/4$	teaspoon basil, crushed
$1/4$	teaspoon freshly ground black pepper or cayenne pepper
$1/4$	teaspoon dry mustard
$1/4$	teaspoon salt

SERVES: 4

Trim fat from steaks; place in baking dish. In small bowl, combine remaining ingredients; mix well. Pour marinade over steaks. Cover; refrigerate 2 hours, turning occasionally.

Remove cooking grids from grill. Preheat grill on high 5 minutes; turn controls to low. Return grids to grill; brush with oil.

Drain steaks, reserving marinade; arrange steaks on grids. Close grill top; grill steaks 8 to 10 minutes on each side or until done, occasionally brushing with marinade.

Cranberry Pork Roast

Grilling Time: 2 to $2^{1}/2$ hours

1	3- to 4-pound pork boneless center loin or sirloin roast, rolled and tied
1	teaspoon freshly ground pepper
1	8-ounce can jellied cranberry sauce
1	teaspoon dry mustard

SERVES: 8 to 10

APRICOT GLAZED PORK: Substitute 1 cup apricot preserves and 2 tablespoons dry white wine for cranberry sauce.

Remove cooking grids from grill; place drip pan on lava rocks in center of grill. Preheat grill on high 5 minutes; turn controls to low.

Rub pepper into roast. Insert spit rod lengthwise through roast. Secure holding forks; check balance. Attach to rotisserie; start motor. Close grill top; spit-roast meat 2 to $2^{1}/2$ hours or until internal temperature reaches 170° F. on meat thermometer.

In small saucepan, melt cranberry sauce over low heat; stir in mustard. During last 20 minutes, frequently brush roast with sauce.

Tenderloin Teriyaki

Grilling Time: 25 to 30 minutes

1	1-pound pork tenderloin
$1/3$	cup chicken broth
2	tablespoons soy sauce
2	tablespoons sherry
2	tablespoons honey
1	clove garlic, minced (optional)
$1/2$	teaspoon grated gingerroot
$1/8$	teaspoon paprika

SERVES: 2 to 3

BARBECUED TENDERLOIN: Substitute Barbecue Sauce (page 14) for marinade.

For even thickness, fold thin end under tenderloin; tie with string. Place tenderloin in baking dish. In small bowl, combine remaining ingredients; mix well. Pour marinade over tenderloin. Cover; refrigerate 4 hours, turning occasionally.

Remove cooking grids from grill. Preheat grill on high 5 minutes; turn controls to low. Return grids to grill; brush with oil.

Drain tenderloin, reserving marinade; place tenderloin on grids. Close grill top; grill tenderloin 25 to 30 minutes or until internal temperature reaches 170° F. on meat thermometer. Place tenderloin on cutting board; with knife slanted, carve tenderloin across the grain into $1/2$-inch slices.

Crown Roast on the Grill

Sprinkle roast with pepper. Wrap bone tips with foil to prevent burning.

Remove cooking grids from grill; place drip pan on lava rocks in center of grill. Preheat grill on high 5 minutes; turn controls to low. Return grids to grill; brush with oil.

Place roast, rib bones up, on grids. Close grill top; grill roast 3½ to 4 hours.

Meanwhile, in large skillet or Dutch oven, sauté celery and onion in butter 5 minutes or until vegetables are crisp-tender. Stir in remaining ingredients. Cover; heat thoroughly, stirring occasionally. After 2 hours, spoon stuffing into center of roast. Close grill top; continue to grill roast 1½ to 2 hours or until internal temperature reaches 170° F. on meat thermometer.

Grilling Time: 3½ to 4 hours

1   *7-pound pork crown roast*
    Freshly ground pepper
1   *cup chopped celery or green pepper*
1   *small onion, finely chopped*
¼   *cup butter or margarine*
4   *cups dry bread cubes*
⅓   *cup chicken broth or water*
2   *apples, peeled, cored, and chopped*
2   *tablespoons chopped parsley*
1   *tablespoon poultry seasoning or ground sage*
1   *teaspoon salt*

SERVES: 14

Lightly cover stuffing with foil if it is browning too rapidly.

Grilled Pork Roast

Trim fat from roast; place in baking dish. In small bowl, combine remaining ingredients; mix well. Pour marinade over roast. Cover; refrigerate 8 hours, turning occasionally.

Remove grids from grill; place drip pan on lava rocks in center of grill. Preheat grill on high 5 minutes; turn controls to low. Return grids to grill; brush with oil.

Drain roast, reserving marinade; place roast, fat side up, on grids. Close grill top; grill roast 2½ to 3 hours or until internal temperature reaches 170° F. on meat thermometer, occasionally brushing with marinade.

Grilling Time: 2½ to 3 hours

1   *4- to 5-pound pork center loin or sirloin roast*
1   *cup apple or pineapple juice*
1   *small onion, finely chopped*
1   *clove garlic, minced (optional)*
1   *teaspoon brown sugar*
1   *teaspoon salt*
½   *teaspoon paprika*
½   *teaspoon freshly ground pepper*
½   *teaspoon thyme, crushed*

SERVES: 6 to 8

Barbecued Pork Roast

Remove cooking grids from grill; place drip pan on lava rocks in center of grill. Preheat grill on high 5 minutes; turn controls to low.

Remove casing from meat; insert spit rod lengthwise through roll. Secure holding forks; check balance. Attach to rotisserie; start motor. Close grill top; spit-roast meat 35 to 45 minutes or until internal temperature reaches 170° F. on meat thermometer. During last 20 minutes, occasionally brush with sauce.

Grilling Time: 35 to 45 minutes

1   *2- to 3-pound pork smoked shoulder roll*
    Mustard Barbecue Sauce (page 14)

SERVES: 6 to 8

1   5-pound fully-cooked canned
    ham
    Dijon mustard
1   cup apple jelly
1/4 cup dry white wine
1   tablespoon prepared
    horseradish
1/8 teaspoon freshly ground
    pepper

SERVES: 10

Apple Glazed Ham

Score ham in 1-inch diamond pattern; lightly rub top surface with mustard.

Remove cooking grids from grill. Preheat grill on high 5 minutes; turn controls to low. Return grids to grill; brush with oil.

Place ham on grids. Close grill top; grill ham 2 hours or until internal temperature reaches 140° F. on meat thermometer. In small saucepan, heat jelly with remaining ingredients until melted. During last 30 minutes, frequently brush ham with glaze. Serve with remaining glaze.

Stud scored ham slice with whole cloves.

Sprinkle brown sugar mixture over ham.

During grilling, sugar mixture will carmelize and glaze the ham.

1   2-pound fully-cooked smoked
    ham center slice, 1 inch
    thick
    Whole cloves (optional)
1/3 cup packed brown sugar
1   teaspoon dry mustard
1/2 teaspoon ground allspice

SERVES: 4 to 6

Glazed Ham Slice

Score one side of ham in 1-inch diamond pattern; insert clove in center of each diamond. In small bowl, combine sugar, mustard, and allspice; mix well. Sprinkle ham with half of sugar mixture.

Remove cooking grids from grill. Preheat grill on high 5 minutes; turn controls to low. Return grids to grill; brush with oil.

Place ham, sugar side up, on grids. Close grill top; grill ham 10 minutes. Turn; sprinkle ham with remaining sugar mixture. Close grill top; continue to grill ham 10 minutes. Discard cloves before serving.

HONEY HAM SLICE: Omit cloves and brown sugar mixture. In small bowl, combine 1/2 cup apple or pineapple juice and 1/2 cup honey; pour over ham in baking dish. Marinate 2 hours, turning occasionally. Drain ham, reserving marinade. Frequently brush ham with marinade during grilling.

Oriental Ribs →

THE BEST

BARBECUED RIBS

Fresh pork back ribs and spareribs are the most popular types for barbecuing and require little advance preparation. You may want the butcher to cut through the ribs at the large end. Country-style ribs can also be barbecued. To reduce cooking time, they can be partially cooked in water before grilling. All types of ribs may be grilled over low heat directly on the grids or on the rotisserie. Two handy accessories for grilling ribs are the Thermos® Broiler Basket for grid-grilling and the Thermos® Chicken/Rib Basket for spit-grilling. For extra flavor, marinate ribs for several hours or brush with a sauce or glaze during grilling. Because of the large amount of bone, allow one pound of ribs per person.

A Thermos® Broiler Basket makes short work of grilling and turning ribs.

Grilling Time: 1 hour

6 pounds pork back ribs or
    spareribs
1¹/₂ cups red wine vinegar
1 6-ounce can frozen pineapple
    concentrate, thawed and
    undiluted
¹/₂ cup packed brown sugar
¹/₄ cup finely chopped green
    pepper
3 tablespoons vegetable oil
2 teaspoons soy sauce
1 clove garlic, minced (optional)

SERVES: 6

Sweet and Sour Ribs

Trim fat from ribs. In small saucepan, combine remaining ingredients. Bring to boil over medium-high heat; reduce heat to low. Simmer 10 minutes, stirring occasionally.

Remove cooking grids from grill; place drip pan on lava rocks in center of grill. Preheat grill on high 5 minutes; turn controls to low. Return grids to grill; brush with oil.

Arrange ribs on grids over drip pan. Close grill top; grill ribs 1 hour or until tender and no longer pink near bone, turning frequently. During last 20 minutes, frequently brush with glaze.

Grilling Time: 1 hour

4 pounds pork back ribs or
    spareribs
¹/₃ cup soy sauce
¹/₄ cup beer
2 tablespoons honey or brown
    sugar
2 tablespoons vegetable oil
1 clove garlic, minced
¹/₂ teaspoon dry mustard
¹/₄ teaspoon ground ginger

SERVES: 4

Oriental Ribs

Trim fat from ribs. In small bowl, combine remaining ingredients; mix well.

Remove cooking grids from grill; place drip pan on lava rocks in center of grill. Preheat grill on high 5 minutes; turn controls to low. Return grids to grill; brush with oil.

Arrange ribs on grids over drip pan. Close grill top; grill ribs 1 hour or until tender and no longer pink near bone, turning frequently. During last 20 minutes, frequently brush with sauce.

BARBECUED RIBS: Substitute ³/₄ cup of your favorite barbecue sauce blended with ¹/₄ cup honey for basting sauce.

Texas Ribs

Trim fat from ribs; sprinkle with black pepper. Place ribs in baking dish. In small bowl, combine remaining ingredients; mix well. Pour marinade over ribs; refrigerate 8 hours, turning occasionally.

Remove cooking grids from grill; place drip pan on lava rocks in center of grill. Preheat grill on high 5 minutes; turn controls to low. Return grids to grill; brush with oil.

Drain ribs, reserving marinade; arrange ribs on grids over drip pan. Close grill top; grill ribs 1 hour or until tender and no longer pink near bone, turning frequently. During last 10 minutes, frequently brush with marinade.

LOUISIANA RIBS: Substitute New Orleans Marinade (page 14) for marinade in recipe.

Grilling Time: 1 hour

4 *pounds pork back ribs or spareribs*
   Freshly ground black pepper
2 *cups tomato juice*
1/4 *cup packed brown sugar or dark corn syrup*
1/4 *cup lemon or lime juice*
2 *tablespoons Worchestershire sauce*
1 *tablespoon chili powder*
2 *teaspoons red pepper flakes*
1 *clove garlic, minced*
1 *teaspoon ground cumin*
1/2 *teaspoon salt*

SERVES: 4

Smoked Ribs

Prepare wood chip log as directed (page 8). Trim fat from ribs. In small bowl, combine remaining ingredients; mix well.

Remove cooking grids from grill. Move lava rocks to right side. Place drip pan opposite rocks on left side of grate; fill with water to 2-inch depth. Preheat grill on high 5 minutes.

Place wood chip log on lava rocks. Close grill top; heat on high 10 to 20 minutes or until chips begin to smolder. Turn controls to low; refill drip pan if necessary. Return cooking grids to grill; brush left grid with oil.

Arrange ribs on left grid; brush with sauce. Close grill top; smoke ribs 2 hours or until tender and no longer pink near bone. During last 30 minutes, frequently brush with sauce. Add more water and wood chip logs, as necessary.

SMOKED BARBECUED RIBS: Substitute your favorite barbecue sauce for sauce in recipe.

Grilling Time: 2 hours

4 *pounds pork back ribs or spareribs*
1/4 *cup Worchestershire sauce*
1/4 *cup butter or margarine, melted*
1/2 *teaspoon salt*
1/4 *teaspoon hot pepper sauce*
1 *clove garlic, minced*

SERVES: 4

4 *pounds pork back ribs or spareribs*
½ *cup ketchup*
⅓ *cup water*
1 *medium onion, finely chopped*
2 *tablespoons vegetable oil*
2 *tablespoons cider vinegar*
1 *tablespoon Worchestershire sauce*
1 *teaspoon chili powder*
½ *teaspoon salt*
¼ *teaspoon freshly ground pepper*

SERVES: 4

Pork Ribs On A Spit

Trim fat from ribs. Thread ribs, accordion style, on spit rod. Secure holding forks; check balance. In small bowl, combine remaining ingredients; mix well.

Remove cooking grids from grill; place drip pan on lava rocks in center of grill. Preheat grill on high 5 minutes; turn controls to low.

Attach spit rod to rotisserie; start motor. Close grill top; grill ribs 1 to 1½ hours or until tender and no longer pink near bone. During last 15 minutes, frequently brush with sauce.

MARINATED RIBS: Before grilling, arrange ribs in baking dish; pour combined sauce ingredients over ribs. Cover; refrigerate 2 to 3 hours, turning occasionally. Drain ribs, reserving marinade. Use marinade as a basting sauce while grilling, as directed in recipe.

4 *pounds pork country-style ribs*
1 *cup apricot preserves*
3 *tablespoons dry white wine*
3 *tablespoons soy sauce*
1 *teaspoon grated gingerroot*
¼ *teaspoon freshly ground pepper*

SERVES: 4

½ teaspoon ground ginger may be substituted for gingerroot.

Grilled Country Ribs

Trim fat from ribs. In small bowl, combine remaining ingredients; mix well.

Remove cooking grids from grill; place drip pan on lava rocks in center of grill. Preheat grill on high 5 minutes; turn controls to low. Return grids to grill; brush with oil.

Arrange ribs on grids over drip pan. Close grill top; grill ribs 45 to 60 minutes or until tender and no longer pink near bone, turning occasionally. During last 15 minutes, frequently brush with sauce. Serve remaining sauce with ribs.

BARBECUED COUNTRY RIBS: Substitute Hot Barbecue Sauce (page 14) for sauce in recipe.

SUPERB SAUSAGE

Bratwurst, thuringer, kielbasa, Italian or Polish sausage, chorizo, and bockwurst are a few of the more than 200 types of sausages available in supermarkets and delicatessens across the country. Whether fresh, smoked, cooked, or uncooked, any sausage that is suitable for indoor cooking can be barbecued on your outdoor gas grill. Of course, the favorites are bratwurst and the all-American frankfurter. When purchasing sausage, be sure to check the package label or consult your butcher to determine whether or not the sausage is uncooked. Uncooked sausage needs thorough cooking, not just heating. If the sausage is precooked or partially cooked, grilling time can be shortened by microwaving or by simmering in a small amount of water. There are many compatible barbecue sauces on the market . . . regular, hot, Cajun, mustard, teriyaki, sweet & sour, and specialty sauces. For more ideas, check the recipes in the "Sauces, Marinades, & More!" chapter (pages 13-15).

Skewered Bratwurst

In small bowl, combine all ingredients, except bratwurst; mix well.

Remove cooking grids from grill. Preheat grill on high 5 minutes; turn controls to low. Return grids to grill; brush with oil.

Thread bratwurst onto long metal skewers; brush with sauce. Arrange kabobs on grids. Close grill top; grill kabobs 8 to 10 minutes or until bratwurst is thoroughly heated, frequently brushing with sauce.

Grilling Time: 8 to 10 minutes

- 1/4 cup half and half
- 2 tablespoons prepared mustard
- 1/2 teaspoon instant minced onion
- 1/2 teaspoon paprika
- 1/4 teaspoon lemon-pepper seasoning
- 6 fully-cooked bratwurst, cut into thirds

SERVES: 6

Brats in Beer

Remove cooking grids from grill. Preheat grill on high 5 minutes; turn controls to medium. Return grids to grill.

In large skillet with heatproof handle, combine bratwurst, beer, and onions; place skillet on grids. Close grill top; bring bratwurst and beer to boil. Turn controls to low. Simmer bratwurst 10 minutes; drain. Brush grids with oil.

Arrange bratwurst on grids. Close grill top; grill bratwurst 6 to 8 minutes, turning occasionally. During last 4 minutes, arrange buns, cut side down, on grids. Serve bratwurst in buns with mustard.

Grilling Time: 16 to 18 minutes

- 8 fresh bratwurst
- 1 12-ounce can beer
- 1 large onion, finely chopped
- 8 frankfurter buns, split German-style mustard

SERVES: 8

Fresh thuringer or bockwurst can be substituted for bratwurst.

Grilling Time: 8 to 10 minutes

4 slices process American cheese
8 frankfurters, slit lengthwise
8 slices bacon
8 frankfurter buns, split
1/4 cup butter or margarine, softened
   Chili sauce
   Pickle relish

SERVES: 8

SWISS BACON DOGS: Substitute 1 cup (4 ounces) shredded Swiss cheese for American cheese and prepared mustard for chili sauce. Omit relish.

Bacon Cheese Dogs

Stack cheese slices; cut into 8 portions. Fill frankfurters with cheese. Wrap bacon slice around each frankfurter; secure with toothpick. Spread cut sides of buns with butter.

Remove cooking grids from grill. Preheat grill on high 5 minutes; turn controls to medium. Return grids to grill; brush with oil.

Arrange frankfurters on grids. Close grill top; grill frankfurters 8 to 10 minutes, turning frequently. During last 4 minutes, arrange buns, cut side down, on grids. Serve frankfurters in buns with chili sauce and relish.

Grilling Time: 6 to 8 minutes

8 frankfurter buns, split
   Butter or margarine, softened
8 frankfurters

SERVES: 8

BARBECUED FRANKS: In small bowl, combine 3/4 cup of your favorite barbecue sauce and 1 tablespoon prepared mustard; mix well. Brush frankfurters with sauce during grilling. Serve with pickle relish.

CHEDDAR FRANKFURTERS: Sprinkle 1 cup (4 ounces) shredded Cheddar cheese on cut sides of grilled buns; grill, cheese side up, until cheese begins to melt.

CHILI DOGS: In small saucepan, heat one 16-ounce can chili on grids; spoon over frankfurters in buns.

Frankfurters

Remove cooking grids from grill. Preheat grill on high 5 minutes; turn controls to medium. Return grids to grill; brush with oil.

Spread cut sides of buns with butter. Arrange frankfurters on grids. Close grill top; grill frankfurters 6 to 8 minutes, turning occasionally. During last 4 minutes, arrange buns, cut side down, on grids. Serve frankfurters in buns with a selection of condiments.

ITALIAN FRANKS: Substitute Italian rolls for buns. Sprinkle 1 cup (4 ounces) shredded mozzarella cheese on cut sides of rolls; grill, cheese side up, until cheese begins to melt. Chop 1 medium onion and 1 green pepper; sauté in 1 tablespoon butter or margarine until crisp-tender. Spoon over frankfurters in buns.

Frankfurters →

LAMB AL FRESCO

Grilling directly on the grill or spit-roasting on the rotisserie are excellent methods for cooking lean tender lamb. To qualify as lamb, not mutton, the meat must come from sheep less than one year old. At this stage, the meat will be delicate in flavor and have a fine velvety texture. Following are a few suggestions for grilling lamb:

AMOUNT: Since most cuts of lamb are lean, 3 to 4 ounces of boneless cooked meat per person are sufficient. Allow a few more ounces for meat with bone. In general, allow the following serving per person:

Chops and Steaks	$1/4$ to $1/3$ pound
Ground Lamb	$1/4$ pound
Roasts, bone-in	$1/3$ to $1/2$ pound
Roasts, boneless	$1/4$ to $1/3$ pound

Most of the recipes in this chapter can be multiplied or divided to accommodate the number of people to be served.

STORAGE: Lamb can be refrigerated in its original wrapping for 4 to 5 days. If the wrapping has been damaged, loosely wrap the meat in waxed paper or foil before storing.

PREPARATION: Although there is generally very little fat on lamb, trim off any excess fat to reduce spattering and to cut calories. Rinse the meat and pat dry with paper towels. The thin paper-like covering (fell) on some cuts of lamb should not be removed, as the fell helps retain the shape of the meat and its juices during grilling.

MARINADES & SAUCES: Like all meat, lamb acquires new flavor appeal when marinated for several hours. Most of the recipes in the chapter "Sauces, Marinades, & More!" (pages 13-15) are delicious with lamb. White Wine Marinade, Curry Marinade, Dijon Mustard Sauce, and Oriental Sauce are just a few of the many selections. Some seasonings particularly suited to lamb are curry powder, mint, ginger, garlic, onion powder, savory, rosemary, dill weed, mustard, and lemon or lime juice. Since lamb is already a tender meat, you do not need to use tenderizers.

GRILLING: Because of the natural tenderness of lamb, lamb chops, steaks, kabobs, and roasts are at their best when cooked by a dry heat method, such as barbecuing. The meat can be grilled or spit-roasted to any degree of doneness that you desire . . . rare (140°F.), medium (160°F.), or well-done (170°F.). Use a meat thermometer for testing roasts. For chops and steaks, make a slit near the bone or in the thickest part of the meat to test doneness. Remember, large cuts of lamb continue to cook after they are removed from the grill. To avoid overcooking, remove meat from the grill when the internal temperature reaches 5 to 10 degrees below the desired serving temperature.

Herbed Lamb Chops →

LAMB GRILLING TIMETABLE

CUT	SIZE/ WEIGHT	DONENESS/ TEMPERATURE	GRILL SETTING	TOTAL TIME*
Chops Loin, Rib, or Shoulder	1 inch thick	Rare Medium Well Done	Medium Medium Medium	12 - 15 minutes 15 - 20 minutes 20 - 25 minutes
	1½ inches thick	Rare Medium Well Done	Medium Medium Medium	15 - 20 minutes 20 - 25 minutes 25 - 30 minutes
Steaks	1 inch thick	Rare Medium Well Done	Medium Medium Medium	12 - 15 minutes 15 - 20 minutes 20 - 25 minutes
	1½ inches thick	Rare Medium Well Done	Medium Medium Medium	15 - 20 minutes 20 - 25 minutes 25 - 30 minutes
Kabobs	1½-inch cubes	Rare Medium Well Done	Low Medium Medium	12 - 15 minutes 15 - 20 minutes 20 - 25 minutes
Roasts Leg, bone-in	5 - 8 pounds	Rare (140° F.) Medium (160° F.) Well Done (170° F.)	Low Low Low	1 ½ - 2 hours 2 - 2 ½ hours 2 ½ - 3 hours
Leg, boneless (Rotisserie)	4 - 6 pounds	Rare (140° F.) Medium (160° F.) Well Done (170°F.)	Low Low Low	1 ½ -2 hours 2 - 2 ½ hours 2 ½ - 3 hours
Crown Roast	6 - 8 pounds	Rare (140° F.) Medium (160° F.) Well Done (170° F.)	Low Low Low	1 ½ - 2 hours 2 - 2 ½ hours 2 ½ - 3 hours

* Approximate grilling time is based on grilling with the grill top closed.

Herbed Lamb Chops

Trim fat from chops; slash edge at 1-inch intervals. Brush chops with lemon juice; sprinkle with basil, garlic powder, and pepper.

Remove cooking grids from grill. Preheat grill on high 5 minutes; turn controls to low. Return grids to grill; brush with oil.

Arrange chops on grids. Close grill top; grill chops 10 to 12 minutes on each side or to desired doneness.

Grilling Time: 20 to 24 minutes

8 lamb loin chops, 1 inch thick
2 tablespoons lemon juice
3/4 teaspoon basil, crushed
1/2 teaspoon garlic powder
1/4 teaspoon freshly ground pepper

SERVES: 4

Curried Lamb Chops

Trim fat from chops; slash edge at 1-inch intervals. Place chops in baking dish. In small bowl, combine remaining ingredients; mix well. Pour over chops. Cover; refrigerate 2 hours, turning occasionally.

Remove cooking grids from grill; place drip pan on lava rocks on right side of grill. Preheat grill on high 5 minutes; turn left control to off and right control to low. Return grids to grill; brush right grid with oil.

Drain chops, reserving marinade; arrange chops on right grid over drip pan. Close grill top; grill chops 10 to 12 minutes on each side or to desired doneness, occasionally brushing with marinade.

Grilling Time: 20 to 24 minutes

4 lamb loin or rib chops, 1 inch thick
1/4 cup dry sherry
2 tablespoons honey
2 tablespoons soy sauce
1 tablespoon grated gingerroot
1 clove garlic, minced (optional)

SERVES: 2

Marinated Sirloin Chops

Trim fat from chops; slash edge at 1-inch intervals. Place chops in baking dish. In small bowl, combine remaining ingredients; mix well. Pour marinade over chops. Cover; refrigerate 2 hours, turning occasionally.

Remove cooking grids from grill; place drip pan on lava rocks on right side of grill. Preheat grill on high 5 minutes; turn left control to off and right control to low. Return grids to grill; brush right grid with oil.

Drain chops, reserving marinade; arrange chops on right grid. Close grill top; grill chops 10 to 15 minutes on each side or to desired doneness, occasionally brushing with marinade.

Grilling Time: 20 to 24 minutes

2 lamb leg sirloin chops, 1 inch thick
1/2 cup apple or grapefruit juice
2 tablespoons honey
2 tablespoons soy sauce
1 tablespoon vegetable oil
1/2 teaspoon paprika
1/2 teaspoon rosemary, crushed
1/4 teaspoon cayenne pepper

SERVES: 2

Pineapple or orange juice may be substituted for apple juice.

Grilling Time: 20 to 24 minutes

4 lamb shoulder chops, 1 inch
   thick
2/3 cup vegetable oil
1/4 cup lemon juice
1 small onion, chopped
1/2 teaspoon lemon-pepper
   seasoning
1/2 teaspoon paprika
1/2 teaspoon salt
1 lemon, sliced
   Parsley sprigs

SERVES: 4

Grilling Time: 25 to 30 minutes

2 pounds lamb shoulder roast,
   boneless, cut into 1¹/₂-inch
   cubes
1 large onion, cut into wedges
   Lemon Herb Marinade
   (page 14)
1 clove garlic, minced
1/2 teaspoon oregano, crushed
1 green pepper, cut into
   1¹/₂-inch squares
12 large mushroom caps
12 cherry tomatoes

SERVES: 6

Lemon Lamb Chops

Arrange chops in baking dish. In small bowl, combine oil, lemon juice, onion, lemon pepper, paprika, and salt. Pour over chops. Cover; refrigerate 4 hours, turning occasionally.

Remove cooking grids from grill; place drip pan on lava rocks in center of grill. Preheat grill on high 5 minutes; turn controls to medium. Return grids to grill; brush with oil.

Drain chops, reserving marinade; arrange chops on grids over drip pan. Close grill top; grill chops 10 to 12 minutes on each side or to desired doneness, occasionally brushing with marinade. Garnish with lemon slices and parsley.

Classic Shish Kabobs

Place meat in baking dish; top with onions. In small bowl, combine marinade, garlic, and oregano; mix well. Pour over meat and onions. Cover; refrigerate 4 hours, turning occasionally.

Remove cooking grids from grill. Preheat grill on high 5 minutes; turn controls to low. Return grids to grill; brush with oil.

Drain meat and onions, reserving marinade. Thread meat onto long metal skewers; alternately thread onion, green pepper, and mushrooms onto skewers; and thread tomatoes onto skewer. Arrange meat kabobs on grids; brush with marinade. Close grill top; grill meat kabobs 25 to 30 minutes, occasionally turning and brushing with marinade.

After 10 minutes, arrange vegetable kabobs, except for tomatoes, on grids. Close grill top; continue to grill 15 to 20 minutes or until vegetables are crisp-tender, occasionally turning and brushing with marinade. During last 5 minutes, grill tomato kabob.

Lamb Patties

In large bowl, combine lamb, curry powder, coriander, onion powder, lemon pepper, and salt; mix lightly. Shape mixture into 4 patties. Wrap bacon slice around edge of each patty; secure with toothpick.

Remove cooking grids from grill. Preheat grill on high 5 minutes; turn left control to off and right control to medium-low. Return grids to grill; brush right grid with oil.

Arrange patties on right grid. Close grill top; grill patties 6 to 8 minutes on each side or until done. Remove toothpicks; serve with sauce.

Grilling Time: 12 to 16 minutes

1	pound ground lamb
1	teaspoon curry powder
1/2	teaspoon ground coriander
1/2	teaspoon onion powder
1/2	teaspoon lemon-pepper seasoning
1/4	teaspoon salt
4	slices bacon
	Lime Honey Sauce (page 15)

SERVES: 4

1/4 pound of ground beef or pork may be substituted for 1/4 pound of lamb.

Barbecued Lamb Loaves

In large bowl, combine all ingredients, except 1/3 cup barbecue sauce; mix lightly. Refrigerate 1 hour. Shape meat mixture into 6 oval loaves.

Remove cooking grids from grill; place drip pan on lava rocks in center of grill. Preheat grill on high 5 minutes; turn controls to low. Return grids to grill; brush with oil.

Arrange loaves on grids over drip pan. Close grill top; grill loaves 20 to 25 minutes or until done, occasionally brushing with remaining sauce during last 15 minutes.

Grilling Time: 20 to 25 minutes

1	pound ground lamb
1/2	pound ground beef
1	cup bottled barbecue sauce, divided
1	cup dry whole-wheat bread crumbs
1	large onion, chopped
1	egg, beaten
1/2	teaspoon oregano, crushed
1/4	teaspoon freshly ground pepper
1/4	teaspoon dry mustard
1/4	teaspoon salt

SERVES: 6

Olympic Burgers

In large bowl, combine meat, crumbs, rosemary, sage, mustard, and pepper; mix lightly. Shape meat mixture into 6 patties, 1/2 inch thick.

Remove cooking grids from grill; place drip pan on lava rocks in center of grill. Preheat grill on high 5 minutes; turn controls to medium-low. Return grids to grill; brush with oil.

Arrange patties on grids over drip pan. Close grill top; grill patties 6 to 8 minutes on each side or until done. During last 8 minutes, arrange onion slices and bread around edge of grids. Serve patties between grilled bread slices with onions and cheese.

Grilling Time: 12 to 16 minutes

1 1/2	pounds ground lamb
1/4	cup dry bread crumbs
1/2	teaspoon rosemary, crushed
1/2	teaspoon ground sage
1/4	teaspoon dry mustard
1/4	teaspoon freshly ground pepper
2	large onions, cut into 1/4-inch slices
12	slices rye bread
1	cup (4 ounces) crumbled feta cheese

SERVES: 6

Grilling Time: 2 to 2½ hours

1   4- to 5-pound lamb shoulder
      roast, boneless
     Freshly ground pepper
     Dry mustard
1   cup bottled barbecue sauce
½   cup apricot preserves

SERVES: 8 to 10

Barbecued Lamb Roast

Remove cooking grids from grill; place drip pan on lava rocks in center of grill. Preheat grill on high 5 minutes; turn controls to medium-low.

Rub roast with pepper and mustard; insert spit rod lengthwise through roast. Secure holding forks; check balance. Attach to rotisserie; start motor. Close grill top; spit-roast meat 2 to 2½ hours or to desired doneness. In small bowl, combine sauce and preserves; mix well. During last 15 minutes, occasionally brush roast with glaze.

ROAST LAMB TERIYAKI: Omit preserves; substitute Teriyaki Marinade (page 13) for barbecue sauce.

Grilling Time: 30 minutes

4   1-pound lamb shanks, cracked
¾   cup white wine
¼   cup honey
2   tablespoons lemon juice
2   tablespoons chopped mint
2   cloves garlic, minced
      (optional)
½   teaspoon lemon-pepper
      seasoning

SERVES: 4 to 6

Grilled Lamb Shanks

Place lamb shanks in 6-quart kettle; cover with water. Bring to boil; reduce heat to low. Cover; simmer 1 hour. Drain lamb; place in large bowl. In small bowl, combine remaining ingredients; mix well. Pour marinade over lamb. Cover; refrigerate 8 hours, turning occasionally.

Remove cooking grids from grill; place drip pan on lava rocks in center of grill. Preheat grill on high 5 minutes; turn controls to medium. Return grids to grill; brush with oil.

Drain lamb, reserving marinade; place lamb on grids over drip pan. Close grill top; grill lamb 30 minutes, occasionally turning and brushing with marinade.

BARBECUED LAMB SHANKS: Substitute Barbecue Sauce (page 14) for marinade.

CRESCENT CITY SHANKS: Substitute New Orleans Marinade (page 14) for marinade.

This unique lamb meal is easy to prepare. After grilling eggplant and lamb patties, simply sandwich lamb between eggplant slices and top with cheese.

Greek Lamb and Eggplant

Cut eggplant crosswise into 8 slices. In large bowl, combine meat, 1/3 cup sauce, bread crumbs, onion, lemon pepper, salt, and savory; mix lightly. Shape meat mixture into 4 patties, similar in size to the eggplant slices.

Remove cooking grids from grill; place drip pan on lava rocks in center of grill. Preheat grill on high 5 minutes; turn controls to medium-low. Return grids to grill; brush with oil.

Brush eggplant with oil; sprinkle with lemon pepper, if desired. Arrange patties and eggplant on grids over drip pan. Close grill top; grill patties 10 to 12 minutes on each side, occasionally brushing with remaining tomato sauce. Place each patty between 2 eggplant slices; top with cheese. Close grill top; grill 2 minutes or until cheese begins to melt.

Grilling Time: 22 to 26 minutes

1	large eggplant
3/4	pound ground lamb
1/4	pound ground beef
1	8-ounce can tomato sauce, divided
1/4	cup dry bread crumbs
1/4	cup finely chopped onion
1/4	teaspoon lemon-pepper seasoning
1/4	teaspoon salt
1/4	teaspoon savory, crushed Vegetable oil
1	cup (4 ounces) shredded mozzarella cheese

SERVES: 4

1   4- to 6-pound lamb leg
    roast, boneless
2/3   cup dry white wine
1/3   cup vegetable oil
2   tablespoons chopped fresh mint
2   tablespoons soy sauce
1   teaspoon dry mustard
1   teaspoon oregano, crushed
1/2   teaspoon rosemary, crushed
1   clove garlic, minced (optional)

SERVES: 8 to 12

Minted Leg of Lamb

With meat mallet or dull edge of French knife, pound meat to even thickness; place meat in baking dish. In small bowl, combine remaining ingredients; mix well. Pour over meat. Cover; refrigerate 8 hours, turning occasionally.

Remove cooking grids from grill; place drip pan on lava rocks in center of grill. Preheat grill on high 5 minutes; turn controls to medium-low. Return grids to grill; brush with oil.

Drain meat, reserving marinade; place meat on grids over drip pan. Close grill top; grill meat 2 to 2½ hours or until tender, occasionally turning and brushing with marinade.

For correct operation of the rotisserie, roasts, whole poultry, and other large cuts of meat, such as this "Stuffed Leg of Lamb" must be balanced so that weight is distributed evenly on the spit rod.

1   4- to 6-pound lamb leg
    roast, boneless
3/4   cup chopped parsley
2   cloves garlic, minced
    (optional)
1   tablespoon oregano, crushed
1   teaspoon grated lemon peel
1/2   teaspoon salt
1/8   teaspoon red pepper flakes
1/4   cup lemon juice

SERVES: 8 to 12

Stuffed Leg of Lamb

Open leg of lamb. In small bowl, combine remaining ingredients, except lemon juice; mix well. Sprinkle mixture into leg opening; close opening. With heavy string, tie leg in several places.

Remove cooking grids from grill; place drip pan on lava rocks in center of grill. Preheat grill on high 5 minutes; turn controls to medium-low.

Insert spit rod lengthwise through lamb. Secure holding forks; check balance. Attach spit rod to rotisserie; start motor. Close grill top; spit-roast lamb 2 to 2½ hours or to desired doneness, occasionally brushing with lemon juice.

SOUTH PACIFIC LAMB: Omit garlic and oregano. In small bowl, combine 1 cup pineapple preserves, ¼ cup dry sherry, and ½ teaspoon curry powder; mix well. During last 20 minutes of grilling, frequently brush meat with glaze.

Oriental Chicken →

THE POULTRY

COOKOUT

All types of poultry are ideally suited to gas grilling. Whether you are cooking on the spit, in the chicken/rib basket, or directly on the grill, the results are marvelously moist and juicy. Also, poultry is so very versatile . . . chicken and turkey especially. Light or dark meat; whole or cut into quarters, halves, legs, thighs, breasts, or wings; marinated or basted with sweet, spicy, or savory mixtures . . . the possibilities are almost endless and always excellent. Before you start grilling, a few reminders may be helpful:

AMOUNT: Since leftover chicken is delicious as is, reheated, cooked in casseroles, or served in salads and sandwiches, it is better to buy too much than too little. Because of the differences in shape and amount of bone, it is somewhat difficult to be precise about the amount of poultry to purchase per person. Following are some general guidelines:

Capons	$1/2$ to $3/4$ pound
Chicken	$1/4$ to $1/2$ chicken, or
	$3/4$ to 1 pound
Cornish Game Hens	$1/2$ large or 1 small hen
Duckling	$3/4$ to 1 pound
Turkey	
11 pounds or less	$3/4$ to 1 pound
12 pounds or more	$1/2$ to $3/4$ pound

Most recipes can easily be multiplied or divided to accommodate the number of people to be served.

PREPARATION: All poultry should be rinsed and patted dry with paper towels before grilling. For whole birds, remember to remove the packets containing the neck, gizzard, and liver from the cavity. These can be used later for gravy, soup, or stuffings. Sprinkle the cavities with salt, pepper, and other herbs.

MARINATING: Although almost any marinade or basting sauce is compatible with poultry, milder versions are best for chickens, capons, and game hens; the more robust types complement duckling and turkey. About 1 to 2 hours is sufficient for marinating small- to medium-sized birds or cut-up parts, since the flavor is primarily on the surface. When feasible, removing the skin will increase flavor penetration. Allow large birds to marinate several hours or even overnight.

TENDERIZING: Since poultry is already tender when properly cooked, there is no need to tenderize it. However, overcooking may toughen the meat.

GRILLING: Poultry is adaptable to direct, basket, or rotisserie grilling. Just follow the recipe directions and the basic principles discussed in the "Great Gas Grilling" chapter. As a general rule, poultry should be grilled at medium to low temperatures. For a crisper skin, turn the poultry midway through grilling period. If grilling without skin, occasionally brush poultry with seasoned melted butter or margarine or with marinade or basting sauce. If the poultry is rather high in fat, like duckling, pierce the skin in many places and grill over a drip pan.

POULTRY GRILLING TIMETABLE

CUT	SIZE/ WEIGHT	GRILL SETTING	TOTAL TIME*
Chicken			
Whole	2 - 3 pounds	Medium-Low	1 - 1¼ hours
Whole, stuffed	2 - 3 pounds	Medium-Low	1¼ - 1½ hours
Halves, Quarters, Pieces	2 - 4 pounds	Medium-Low	40 - 50 minutes
Cornish Hens	1½ pounds	Low	35 - 50 minutes
Duckling			
Whole	3 - 5 pounds	Medium-Low	1½ - 2 hours
Whole, stuffed	3 - 5 pounds	Medium-Low	2 - 2½ hours
Turkey			
Whole	10 - 14 pounds	Low	3½ - 4½ hours
Whole, stuffed	10 - 14 pounds	Low	4¼ - 6 hours
Halves, Quarters, Pieces	4 - 6 pounds	Low	50 - 55 minutes

* Approximate grilling time is based on grilling with the grill top closed.

Oriental Chicken

Grilling Time: 40 to 50 minutes

Arrange chicken in baking dish. In small bowl, combine remaining ingredients; mix well. Pour marinade over chicken. Cover; refrigerate 4 hours or more, turning occasionally.

    Remove cooking grids from grill. Preheat grill on high 5 minutes; turn left control to off and right control to medium-low. Return grids to grill; brush right grid with oil.

    Drain chicken, reserving marinade; arrange chicken on right grid. Close grill top; grill chicken 40 to 50 minutes or until tender, occasionally brushing with marinade.

CHICKEN WITH PLUM SAUCE: Substitute ⅓ cup plum sauce for soy sauce and sherry.

- 4 *chicken legs with thighs*
- ⅓ *cup vegetable oil*
- ⅓ *cup sliced green onions*
- ¼ *cup honey*
- ¼ *cup soy sauce*
- 2 *tablespoons dry sherry*
- 1 *teaspoon grated gingerroot*
- 1 *clove garlic, minced (optional)*

SERVES: 4 to 6

½ teaspoon ground ginger may be substituted for gingerroot.

Grilled Chicken

1   cup butter or margarine
1   teaspoon lemon-pepper
    seasoning
1   teaspoon paprika
2   2^1/$_2$- to 3-pound broiler-fryer
    chickens, halved or
    quartered

SERVES: 4 to 6

In small saucepan, combine butter, lemon pepper, and paprika; heat thoroughly over low heat.

Remove cooking grids from grill. Preheat grill on high 5 minutes; turn controls to medium-low. Return grids to grill; brush with oil.

Brush chicken with sauce; arrange chicken, skin side up, on grids. Close grill top; grill chicken 40 to 50 minutes or until tender, occasionally brushing with sauce.

PARMESAN CHICKEN: Add ^{1}/$_4$ cup (2 ounces) grated Parmesan cheese and ^{1}/$_2$ teaspoon basil, crushed, to basting sauce.

Barbecued Chicken

2   2^1/$_2$- to 3-pound broiler-fryer
    chickens, cut up
    Barbecue Sauce (page 14)

SERVES: 4 to 6

Remove cooking grids from grill. Preheat grill on high 5 minutes; turn controls to medium-low. Return grids to grill; brush with oil.

Brush chicken with sauce; arrange chicken, skin side up, on grids. Close grill top; grill chicken 40 to 50 minutes or until tender, occasionally brushing with sauce.

EASY BARBECUED CHICKEN: Substitute your favorite bottled barbecue sauce for Barbecue Sauce.

Lemon Chicken

2   2^1/$_2$- to 3-pound broiler-fryer
    chickens, halved or
    quartered
^{1}/$_2$ cup dry white wine
^{1}/$_4$ cup lemon juice
^{1}/$_4$ cup vegetable oil
^{1}/$_2$ teaspoon freshly ground
    pepper
^{1}/$_4$ teaspoon dry mustard

SERVES: 4 to 6

Arrange chicken in baking dish. In small bowl, combine remaining ingredients; mix well. Pour marinade over chicken. Cover; refrigerate 4 hours or more, turning occasionally.

Remove cooking grids from grill. Preheat grill on high 5 minutes; turn controls to medium-low. Return grids to grill; brush with oil.

Drain chicken, reserving marinade; arrange chicken, skin side up, on grids. Close grill top; grill chicken 40 to 50 minutes or until tender, occasionally brushing with marinade.

BURGUNDY CHICKEN: Substitute Burgundy or other dry red wine for white wine and lemon juice; add ^{1}/$_4$ teaspoon tarragon, crushed.

Sherried Chicken

Arrange chicken in baking dish. In small bowl, combine remaining ingredients; mix well. Pour marinade over chicken. Cover; refrigerate 4 hours or more, turning occasionally.

Remove cooking grids from grill. Preheat grill on high 5 minutes; turn controls to medium-low. Return grids to grill; brush with oil.

Drain chicken, reserving marinade; arrange chicken, skin side up, on grill. Close grill top; grill chicken 40 to 50 minutes or until tender, occasionally brushing with marinade.

SHERRIED GAME HENS: Substitute 2 to 3 Cornish game hens, halved, for chickens. Omit garlic.

2	2^1/2- to 3-pound broiler-fryer chickens, quartered
1	cup dry sherry
^{1}/2	cup vegetable oil
1	medium onion, minced
1	tablespoon Worchestershire sauce
1	clove garlic, minced
1	teaspoon lemon juice
1	teaspoon rosemary, crushed
1	teaspoon soy sauce

SERVES: 4 to 6

Tarragon Chicken

In small bowl, combine all ingredients, except chicken; mix well. Rub small amount of mixture on chicken; heat remaining mixture for basting sauce.

Remove cooking grids from grill. Preheat grill on high 5 minutes; turn left control to off and right control to medium-low. Return grids to grill; brush right grid with oil.

Arrange chicken on right grid. Close grill top; grill chicken 40 to 50 minutes or until tender, occasionally brushing with sauce.

^{1}/2	cup butter or margarine, softened
2	tablespoons lemon juice
1	to 2 tablespoons tarragon, crushed
1	teaspoon Dijon mustard
1	2^1/2-to 3-pound broiler-fryer chicken, cut up

SERVES: 2 to 3

Brandied Chicken

In small saucepan, combine all ingredients, except chicken and peaches; heat thoroughly over medium heat until sugar dissolves.

Remove cooking grids from grill. Preheat grill on high 5 minutes; turn controls to medium-low. Return grids to grill; brush with oil.

Brush chicken with sauce; arrange chicken, skin side up, on grids. Close grill top; grill chicken 40 to 50 minutes or until tender, occasionally brushing with sauce. During last 10 minutes, grill peaches, occasionally brushing with sauce.

^{1}/2	cup butter or margarine
^{1}/4	cup brandy
^{1}/4	cup packed brown sugar
^{1}/4	cup lemon juice
2	2^1/2-to 3-pound broiler-fryer chickens, halved
4	peaches, peeled, halved, and pitted

SERVES: 4 to 6

Firm, canned peach halves may be substituted for fresh peaches.

Grilling Time: 1 to 1½ hours

6 chicken thighs
3 chicken breasts, halved
½ cup vegetable oil
½ cup cider vinegar
½ teaspoon basil, crushed
¼ teaspoon salt
¼ teaspoon cayenne pepper

SERVES: 4 to 6

Chicken in a Basket

Arrange chicken in baking dish. In a small bowl, combine remaining ingredients; mix well. Pour marinade over chicken. Cover; refrigerate 3 hours, turning occasionally.

Remove cooking grids from grill; place drip pan on lava rocks in center of grill. Preheat grill on high 5 minutes; turn controls to medium.

Brush Chicken/Rib Basket with oil; center on spit rod. Drain chicken; layer in basket, filling two-thirds full. Check balance. Attach spit rod to rotisserie, centering basket over drip pan; start motor. Close grill top; spit-roast chicken 1 to 1½ hours or until tender.

Grilling Time: 6 to 8 minutes

2 chicken breasts, boned,
    skinned, and halved
1 teaspoon basil, crushed
1 teaspoon freshly ground black
    pepper
1 teaspoon oregano, crushed
1 teaspoon paprika
½ teaspoon sugar
¼ teaspoon cayenne pepper
¼ teaspoon salt
¼ teaspoon savory
¼ cup butter or margarine,
    melted

SERVES: 2 to 4

Although the chicken will be almost black on the outside, it will be moist and tender inside. Be sure to use very heavy hot pan mitts when handling the skillet. It is best to let the skillet cool on the grill after using.

Cajun Blackened Chicken

With meat mallet or dull edge of French knife, pound chicken to ¼-inch thickness. In small bowl, combine remaining ingredients, except butter; mix well. Brush chicken with butter; coat with seasoning mixture. Arrange chicken in baking dish; refrigerate 20 to 30 minutes or until ready to cook.

Remove cooking grids from grill. Preheat grill on high 5 minutes. Return grids to grill. Place large iron skillet on grids. Close grill top; heat skillet on high 20 to 30 minutes until very hot.

Quickly arrange chicken in skillet; cook 3 to 4 minutes on each side or until tender.

GRILLED BLACKENED CHICKEN: Substitute 2 teaspoons Italian herb seasoning for basil, oregano, and salt. Omit skillet; brush grids with oil. With grill top closed, grill chicken directly on grids at medium-high temperature for 2 to 3 minutes on each side or until tender.

CAJUN BLACKENED CHICKEN . . .
It's Not All Smoke

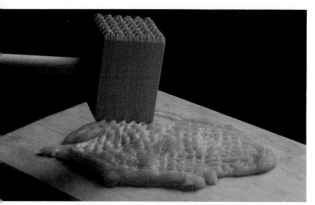

Pound chicken breasts to ¹/₄-inch thickness.

Coat chicken with seasoning mixture.

Adding chilled chicken to a very hot skillet creates a lot of smoke. This makes blackened chicken and similar blackened recipes ideal for outdoor cooking.

½ cup butter or margarine,
     softened
1 teaspoon curry powder
1 teaspoon finely chopped
     parsley
½ teaspoon cayenne pepper
4 chicken breasts, halved

SERVES: 6 to 8

Chicken breasts can be skinned and boned, if desired.

Curried Chicken Breasts

In small bowl, combine all ingredients, except chicken; mix well. Rub mixture on chicken.

Remove cooking grids from grill; place drip pan on lava rocks in center of grill. Preheat grill on high 5 minutes; turn controls to medium.

Brush Flat Rotisserie Basket with oil; layer chicken in basket. Center basket on spit rod; check balance. Attach spit rod to rotisserie, centering basket over drip pan; start motor. Close grill top; spit-roast breasts 1 to 1½ hours or until tender.

The Thermos® Flat Rotisserie Basket makes simple work of turning the chicken for you.

A large paper or plastic bag is ideal for coating chicken wings with seasonings.

Grilling Time: 16 to 20 minutes

2 teaspoons paprika
1 teaspoon lemon-pepper
     seasoning
1 teaspoon onion powder
½ teaspoon salt
½ teaspoon red pepper flakes
½ teaspoon sage
3 pounds chicken wings, tips
     removed

SERVES: 4

Spiced Chicken Wings

In large paper or plastic bag, combine all ingredients, except chicken wings. Add wings, a few at a time; shake to coat with seasonings. Place wings in baking dish. Cover; refrigerate 1 hour.

Remove cooking grids from grill. Preheat grill on high 5 minutes; turn left control to off and right control to low. Return cooking grids to grill; brush right grid with oil.

Arrange wings on right grid. Close grill top; grill wings 8 to 10 minutes on each side or until tender.

Smoked Capon

Prepare wood chip log as directed (page 8). Remove neck and giblets from capon; discard or save for use in gravy or soup. Rinse capon; pat dry with paper towels. Sprinkle cavity with salt; fill with celery, onion, and parsley. With heavy string, tie legs and wings to capon; close neck opening with small skewer.

Remove cooking grids from grill. Move lava rocks to right side. Place drip pan opposite rocks on left side of grate; fill with water to 2-inch depth. Preheat grill on high 5 minutes.

Place wood chip log on lava rocks. Close grill top; heat 10 to 20 minutes or until chips begin to smolder. Turn controls to low. Using basting bulb, refill drip pan if necessary. Return grids to grill; brush with oil.

Place capon on grid over drip pan. Close grill top; smoke capon 2¹/₂ to 3 hours or until tender. Add more water and wood chip logs, as necessary. Discard vegetables before serving.

Smoked poultry is slightly pinker near the bone than poultry roasted in the conventional manner.

A Thermos® Grill Smoker filled with soaked wood chips is an excellent alternative to the wood chip log. Refer to use directions on page 8.

Grilling Time: 2¹/₂ to 3 hours

1   5-to 7-pound capon or
       roasting chicken
     Salt
1   stalk celery with leaves, cut
       into chunks
1   small onion, sliced
¹/₄   cup parsley sprigs

SERVES: 6 to 8

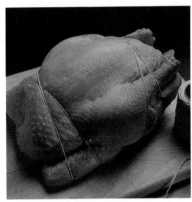

All poultry must be tied securely for use on the rotisserie. This prevents legs and wings from flopping.

Chicken on a Spit

Remove neck and giblets from chicken; discard or save for use in gravy or soup. Rinse chicken; pat dry with paper towels. In large skillet, sauté onions and garlic in butter or until onions are tender. Add sausage and thyme; cook 5 minutes, stirring constantly. Stir in remaining ingredients.

Lightly stuff chicken cavity; secure with small skewers. With heavy string, tie legs and wings to chicken. Close neck opening with small skewers.

Remove cooking grids from grill. Place drip pan on lava rocks in center of grill. Preheat grill on high 5 minutes; turn controls to low.

Insert spit rod lengthwise through chicken. Secure holding forks; check balance. Attach to rotisserie; start motor. Close grill top; spit-roast chicken 1¹/₂ hours or until tender.

Allow 15 minutes per pound when roasting chickens that are not stuffed.

Grilling Time: 1¹/₂ hours

1   4-to 5-pound roasting
       chicken or capon
2   medium onions, finely
       chopped
2   cloves garlic, minced
       (optional)
¹/₄   cup butter or margarine
¹/₂   pound ground pork sausage
1   teaspoon thyme, crushed
1¹/₂   cups coarse dry bread crumbs
¹/₃   cup chopped parsley
¹/₂   teaspoon salt
     Freshly ground pepper
2   eggs, beaten

SERVES: 4 to 6

Savory Stuffed Chicken: Omit garlic and thyme; sauté 1 medium apple, peeled, cored, and chopped, with onions. Add 1 teaspoon poultry seasonings to stuffing.

Mexican Chicken

In small saucepan, combine butter, chili powder, oregano, and cayenne; heat thoroughly over low heat.

Remove cooking grids from grill. Preheat grill on high 5 minutes; turn controls to medium-low. Return grids to grill; brush with oil.

Brush chicken with sauce; arrange chicken, skin side up, on grids. Close grill top; grill chicken 40 to 50 minutes or until tender, occasionally brushing with sauce. During last 10 minutes, grill pepper rings, occasionally brushing with sauce. Serve on chicken.

Grilling Time: 40 to 50 minutes

- 1/4 cup butter or margarine
- 1 tablespoon chili powder
- 1/2 teaspoon oregano, crushed
- 1/8 teaspoon cayenne pepper
- 4 chicken legs with thighs
- 2 large green peppers, cut into rings

SERVES: 4

Four chicken breasts can be substituted for chicken legs with thighs.

Orange Glazed Duckling

Remove neck and giblets from duckling; discard or save for use in gravy or soup. Rinse duckling; pat dry with paper towels. With heavy string, tie legs and wings to duckling. Close neck opening with small skewers. With fork, pierce skin in many places. In small saucepan, combine remaining ingredients; heat thoroughly over low heat.

Remove cooking grids from grill; place drip pan on lava rocks in center of grill. Preheat grill on high 5 minutes; turn controls to low. Return grids to grill; brush with oil.

Place duckling, breast side up, on cooking grids over drip pan. Close grill top; grill duckling 2 to 2½ hours or until tender. During last 15 minutes, occasionally brush with glaze. Empty drip pan, as necessary.

Grilling Time: 2 to 2½ hours

- 1 4½-to 5-pound duckling
- 1/2 cup orange marmalade
- 2 tablespoons orange-flavored liqueur
- 2 tablespoons soy sauce
- 1/2 teaspoon basil or rosemary, crushed

SERVES: 2 to 3

Sherry Duckling: Substitute 2 tablespoons dry sherry for liqueur in glaze; add ½ teaspoon dry mustard.

Herb Duckling

With fork, pierce duckling skin in many places. In small bowl, combine remaining ingredients; mix well.

Remove cooking grids from grill; place large drip pan on lava rocks in center of grill. Preheat grill on high 5 minutes; turn controls to low. Return grids to grill; brush with oil.

Place duckling halves, skin side up, on grids over drip pan. Close grill top; grill duckling 1 to 1½ hours or until tender, occasionally brushing with sauce. Empty drip pan, as necessary.

Photograph on page 66 shows Herb Duckling prepared to serve 4.

Grilling Time: 1 to 1½ hours

- 1 4½-to 5-pound duckling, halved
- 1/4 cup vegetable oil
- 1/2 teaspoon basil, crushed
- 1/2 teaspoon oregano, crushed
- 1/2 teaspoon paprika
- 1/2 teaspoon salt
- 1/4 teaspoon dry mustard
- 1/4 teaspoon freshly ground pepper

SERVES: 2

For a crisper skin, score skin in 1-inch diamond pattern before grilling. Turn duckling, skin side down, after 30 minutes.

← **Herb Duckling**

1 5-to 6-pound duckling
   Oriental Sauce (page 15)
   Apple, cored and quartered

SERVES: 3 to 4

A Thermos® Grill Smoker filled with soaked wood chips is an excellent alternative to the wood chip log. Refer to directions on (page 8).

SMOKED DUCKLING ITALIANO: Substitute clear Italian dressing for Oriental Sauce.

Smoked Duckling

Place duckling in baking dish; pour sauce over duckling. Cover; refrigerate 8 hours, turning occasionally.

Prepare wood chip log as directed (page 8). Remove cooking grids from grill. Move lava rocks to right side. Place drip pan opposite rocks on left side of grate; fill with water to 2-inch depth. Preheat grill on high 5 minutes.

Place wood chip log on lava rocks. Close grill top; heat on high 10 to 20 minutes or until chips begin to smolder. Turn controls to low. Using basting bulb, refill drip pan if necessary. Return grids to grill; brush left grid with oil.

Drain duckling, reserving marinade. With fork, pierce skin in many places; fill cavity with apple. With heavy string, tie legs and wings to duckling; close neck opening with small skewers.

Place duckling on left grid over drip pan. Close grill top; smoke duckling 3 to 3½ hours or until tender, occasionally brushing with marinade. Add more water and wood chip logs, as necessary. Empty drip pan, as necessary. Discard apple before serving. Serve duckling with Ginger Orange Sauce (page 15), if desired.

1 4-to 5-pound capon or
   roasting chicken
   Teriyaki Marinade (page 13)

SERVES: 4

LOUISIANA CAPON: Substitute New Orleans Marinade (page 15) for Teriyaki Marinade.

Teriyaki Capon

Remove neck and giblets from capon; discard or save for gravy or soup. Rinse capon; pat dry with paper towels. Place in baking dish. Pour marinade over capon. Cover; refrigerate 4 hours, turning occasionally.

Remove cooking grids from grill; place drip pan on lava rocks in center of grill. Preheat grill on high 5 minutes; turn controls to low.

Drain capon, reserving marinade. With heavy string, tie legs and wings to capon. Insert spit rod lengthwise through capon. Secure holding forks; check balance. Attach to rotisserie; start motor. Close grill top; spit-roast capon 1½ to 2 hours or until tender, occasionally brushing with marinade.

Grilled Game Hens

Grilling Time: 45 to 50 minutes

Remove cooking grids from grill. Preheat grill on high 5 minutes; turn controls to medium-low. Return grids to grill; brush with oil.

Brush hens with butter; sprinkle with seasoning. Arrange hens, skin side up, on grids. Close grill top; grill hens 45 to 50 minutes, occasionally brushing with butter. Brush cut side of tomatoes with butter; sprinkle with seasoning and cheese. During last 10 minutes, grill tomatoes.

SAVORY GAME HENS: Substitute $1/2$ teaspoon rosemary, crushed, and $1/4$ teaspoon cayenne pepper for lemon-pepper seasoning.

2	*Cornish game hens, halved*
$1/3$	*cup butter or margarine, melted*
	Lemon-pepper seasoning
4	*large firm tomatoes, halved*
	Shredded Cheddar cheese

SERVES: 3 to 4

Glazed Cornish Hens

Grilling Time: 45 to 50 minutes

In small bowl, combine butter, chives, and rosemary; mix well. Rub small amount of mixture on hens; heat remaining mixture for basting sauce. In small saucepan, combine jam and wine; heat thoroughly over low heat.

Remove cooking grids from grill; place drip pan on lava rocks in center of grill. Preheat grill on high 5 minutes; turn controls to low. Return grids to grill; brush with oil.

Arrange hens, skin side up, on grids over drip pan. Close grill top; grill hens 45 to 50 minutes or until tender, occasionally basting with sauce. During last 10 minutes, occasionally brush hens with jam glaze. To serve, garnish with apricot halves and watercress.

CORNISH HENS A L'ORANGE: Omit chives and apricot halves. Substitute $1/4$ cup orange marmalade for jam and 2 tablespoons orange-flavored liqueur for wine.

SOUTHERN GAME HENS: Omit chives and apricot halves. Substitute bourbon for wine in glaze; add 1 teaspoon soy sauce.

$1/2$	*cup butter or margarine, softened*
2	*tablespoons chopped chives*
$1/2$	*teaspoon rosemary, crushed*
4	*Cornish game hens, halved*
$1/4$	*cup apricot jam*
2	*tablespoons dry white wine or dry sherry*
8	*fresh or canned apricot halves*
	Watercress

SERVES: 8

For a festive touch Cornish hens can be served with rice pilaf or a combination of white and wild rice.

1 5½-to 6-pound turkey breast,
   bone in
   Hot Teriyaki Sauce (page 13)

SERVES: 8 to 10

Smoked turkey is delicious served chilled. In fact, refrigerating overnight intensifies the smoked flavor.

SMOKED BARBECUED TURKEY: Substitute Barbecue Sauce (page 14) or Mustard Barbecue Sauce (page 14) for Hot Teriyaki Sauce.

Smoked Teriyaki Turkey

Rinse turkey; pat dry with paper towels. Place in baking dish; pour sauce over turkey. Cover; refrigerate 8 hours, turning occasionally.

Prepare wood chip log as directed (page 8). Remove cooking grids from grill. Move lava rocks to right side. Place drip pan opposite rocks on left side of grate; fill with water to 2-inch depth. Preheat grill on high 5 minutes.

Place wood chip log on lava rocks. Close grill top; heat on high 10 to 20 minutes or until chips begin to smolder. Turn left control to off and right control to low. Using basting bulb, refill drip pan if necessary. Return grids to grill; brush left grid with oil.

Drain turkey, reserving marinade. Place turkey on left grid over drip pan. Close grill top; smoke turkey 2½ to 3 hours or until tender, brushing with sauce every 30 minutes. Add more water and wood chip logs, as necessary.

1 8-to 10-pound turkey
   Freshly ground pepper
   Salt
1 large onion, sliced
1 bunch parsley
1 clove garlic, halved (optional)
   Butter or margarine
   Paprika

SERVES: 8 to 10

Turkey on a Spit

Remove neck and giblets from turkey; discard or save for use in gravy or soup. Rinse turkey; pat dry with paper towels. Sprinkle turkey cavity with pepper and salt; fill cavity with onion, parsley, and garlic. Rub skin with small amount of butter; sprinkle with paprika. With heavy string, tie legs and wings to turkey; close neck opening with small skewer.

Remove cooking grids from grill. Place drip pan on lava rocks in center of grill; fill with water to 2-inch depth. Preheat grill on high 5 minutes; turn controls to low.

Insert spit rod lengthwise through turkey. Secure holding forks; check balance. Attach to rotisserie; start motor.

Close grill top; spit-roast turkey 3 to 4 hours or until center of thigh registers 180° F. on meat thermometer. If legs and wings are browning too rapidly, cover with foil. Using basting bulb, add more water, as necessary. Let turkey stand 10 to 20 minutes before carving. Discard onion, parsley, and garlic before serving.

Swordfish Jardiniere (page 75) →

SENSATIONAL SEAFOOD

There are two types of seafood, fish and shellfish, and more than a hundred varieties are available in supermarkets across the nation. These include such favorites as cod, mackerel, halibut, haddock, trout, orange roughy, red snapper, tuna, swordfish, salmon, and many more. Although the types of fish available may vary with the season and the region, there is always a wide variety from which to choose. Also, many of the fish are interchangeable in recipes. The most popular shellfish for grilling are shrimp, scallops, and lobster. Grilled seafood can be enjoyed the year 'round, and the transition from conventional cooking to barbecuing on a gas grill is minimal. Here are a few tips for preparing and grilling seafood with ease:

PURCHASING TIPS & AMOUNTS: Fresh or frozen fish can be purchased in several forms . . . fillets, steaks, or whole, drawn or dressed. Fillets are lengthwise slices from the sides of a fish, and steaks are the crosscut slices from large fish. Drawn whole fish have the entrails and scales removed, but not the bones. Dressed whole fish have the entrails, fins, and scales removed.

Shrimp are available raw or cooked in the shell or shelled and deveined. They range in size from jumbo (15 or fewer per pound) to small (42 or more per pound). Lobster is sold live or as frozen tails (2 to 8 ounces). Large sea scallops are the most practical for grilling, although small bay scallops can be cooked on the grill in foil bundles or sautéed in a skillet.

When purchasing fish or shellfish, allow these amounts for each person:

Fish fillets or steaks	1/4 to 1/3 pound
Whole fish, drawn	3/4 to 1 pound
Whole fish, dressed	1/2 to 3/4 pound
Shrimp in the shell	1/3 to 1/2 pound
Shrimp, shelled and deveined	1/4 to 1/3 pound
Scallops	1/4 to 1/3 pound
Lobster tails	6- to 8-ounce tail

STORAGE: Fresh seafood should be refrigerated immediately after purchasing and cooked the same day, if possible. Frozen seafood can be stored in the freezer for several months. Once seafood has been thawed, it should not be refrozen.

PREPARATION: Depending on which form is purchased, most seafood requires very little preparation. Simply rinse the seafood and pat dry with paper towels. To clean shrimp in the shell, remove the shell; then, make a shallow cut along the outer rim of the shrimp and remove the back vein. Since fish fillets and steaks vary according to the size of the fish, you may want to cut large pieces into single portions before grilling.

MARINADES & SAUCES: Even strong-flavored seafood is relatively mild when compared to meat; therefore, delicately-flavored marinades and sauces are the most compatible. Exceptions are Cajun seasonings and teriyaki-type marinades and sauces, which blend beautifully with a variety of fish and shellfish, especially red snapper, red fish, cod, halibut, shrimp, and lobster. Many of the recipes in the "Sauces, Marinades, & More" chapter (pages 13-15) are perfectly suited to seafood, including New Orleans Marinade, White Wine Marinade, Dill Cream Sauce, Lime Honey Sauce, and Curry Butter. There are several seasonings that enhance fish and shellfish . . . curry powder, dill, basil, rosemary, tarragon, and thyme.

GRILLING: As a general rule, allow 10 minutes per inch of thickness when cooking fish. Measure the fish at its thickest part to estimate grilling time. Since fish is very lean, be sure the grids have been brushed with oil to prevent sticking. The Fish Broiler and Broiler Basket made by Thermos® are useful tools for grilling whole fish, fillets, or steaks. The baskets hold the fish together, and the long handles facilitate turning. Shrimp and scallops can be threaded onto skewers, wrapped in foil bundles with other ingredients, or sautéed in a skillet or flat-bottomed wok. These shellfish cook very quickly, so be careful not to overcook. Lobster tails can be grilled directly on the grids, occasionally brushing with basting sauce.

Mackerel, red snapper, salmon, striped bass, and whitefish are excellent fish for stuffing. Here a stuffed white-fish is ready for the grill.

Grilled Stuffed Fish

Grilling Time: 45 to 50 minutes

Rinse fish; pat dry with paper towels. Brush large sheet of heavy-duty foil with vegetable oil; place fish on foil. In large skillet, sauté green pepper, onion, basil, salt, and tarragon in butter until vegetables are crisp-tender. Stir in rice and mushrooms. Fill fish with rice mixture; brush with oil. Top with lemon slices.

Remove cooking grids from grill. Preheat grill on high 5 minutes; turn controls to low. Return grids to grill.

Place foil with fish on grids. Close grill top; grill fish 45 to 50 minutes or until fish flakes easily with fork.

1	3- to 4-pound dressed whole fish
	Vegetable oil
1/3	cup chopped green pepper
1/3	cup chopped onion
1/2	teaspoon basil, crushed
1/2	teaspoon salt
1/2	teaspoon tarragon, crushed
1/4	cup butter or margarine
1 1/2	cups cooked rice
1	cup sliced mushrooms
1	lemon, sliced

SERVES: 6 to 8

1/4 cup butter or margarine
  1 tablespoon lemon or lime
     juice
1/4 teaspoon cayenne pepper
1 1/2 pounds salmon steaks, 1 inch
     thick
1/3 cup cracked peppercorns
  1 lemon or lime, thinly sliced

SERVES: 4 to 5

**Cod, swordfish, or tuna steaks
may be substituted for salmon.**

*Fresh pepper enhances the flavor
of most fish. Used here with salmon
steaks, cracked peppercorns are
pressed directly into the fish for an
even more pronounced flavor.*

Pepper Fish Steaks

In small saucepan, combine butter, lemon juice, and cayenne; heat thoroughly over low heat. Brush steaks with butter mixture; press peppercorns into both sides of steaks.

Remove cooking grids from grill. Preheat grill on high 5 minutes; turn controls to medium-low. Return grids to grill; brush with oil.

Arrange steaks on grids. Close grill top; grill steaks 5 to 6 minutes on each side or until fish flakes easily with fork. To serve, garnish steaks with lemon slices.

Curried Cod Fillets

1/4 cup sliced green onion
  1 teaspoon curry powder
1/4 teaspoon dried red pepper
     flakes
1/8 teaspoon cayenne pepper
1/4 teaspoon sugar
1/4 cup butter or margarine
  2 teaspoons lemon juice
  1 pound cod fillets

SERVES: 2 to 3

**Grouper, orange roughy, sole,
or white fish fillets may be
substituted for cod.**

In small skillet, sauté green onion, curry, red pepper flakes, cayenne, and sugar in butter; stir in lemon juice.

Remove cooking grids from grill. Preheat grill on high 5 minutes; turn controls to medium-low. Return grids to grill; brush with oil.

Brush fillets with butter sauce; arrange fillets on grids. Close grill top; grill fillets 10 to 12 minutes or until fish flakes easily with fork, occasionally brushing with sauce. Spoon any remaining sauce over fillets before serving.

**To facilitate turning, fillets can be grilled in a
Thermos® Broiler Basket that has been brushed with
vegetable oil.**

Orange Roughy Milanese

Grilling Time: 10 to 12 minutes

Divide fillets among four squares of heavy-duty foil. In small bowl, combine remaining ingredients; mix lightly. Spoon mixture over fillets. Bring together four corners of each square; twist to close packet.

Remove cooking grids from grill. Preheat grill on high 5 minutes; turn controls to medium-low. Return grids to grill.

Arrange foil packets on grill. Close grill top; grill fillets 10 to 12 minutes or until fish flakes easily with fork.

$1^1/_2$ pounds orange roughy fillets
1   cup chopped peeled tomato
2   tablespoons Italian dressing
2   tablespoons finely chopped onion
1   teaspoon basil, crushed
1   tablespoon lemon or lime juice
1   tablespoon chopped parsley
$^1/_4$ teaspoon cayenne pepper

SERVES: 4 to 5

Swordfish Jardiniere

Grilling Time: 10 to 12 minutes

In small saucepan, combine butter, lemon juice, mustard, and pepper; heat thoroughly over low heat. Brush large sheet of heavy-duty foil with butter mixture; arrange steaks in center of foil. Pour remaining butter mixture over steaks. Top with carrots, dill, and parsley. Bring long sides of foil together; double fold sides and ends of foil.

Remove cooking grids from grill. Preheat grill on high 5 minutes; turn controls to medium-low. Return grids to grill.

Arrange foil packet on grids. Close grill top; grill steaks 10 to 12 minutes or until fish flakes easily with fork.

Red snapper, seabass, flounder, grouper, orange roughy, or scrod fillets may be substituted for swordfish.

$^1/_3$ cup butter
1   tablespoon lemon juice
$^1/_4$ teaspoon dry mustard
$^1/_4$ teaspoon freshly ground pepper
2   pounds swordfish steaks
$^1/_2$ cup shredded carrots or carrot ribbons
$^3/_4$ teaspoon dill weed
1   tablespoon finely chopped parsley (optional)

SERVES: 6

Grilled Flounder Fillets

Grilling Time: 10 to 20 minutes

Rub fillets with one lemon half. In small bowl, combine celery, onion, parsley, salt, oregano, and pepper; mix well. Sprinkle mixture on both sides of fillets. Combine nuts and butter.

Remove cooking grids from grill. Preheat grill on high 5 minutes; turn controls to medium-low. Return grids to grill; brush with oil.

Squeeze remaining lemon half over fillets; arrange fillets on grids. Close grill top; grill fillets 10 to 12 minutes or until fish flakes easily with fork. During last 5 minutes, sprinkle nuts over fillets.

Bass, cod, sole, or other white fish fillets may be substituted for flounder.

2   pounds flounder fillets
1   lemon, halved
2   tablespoons finely chopped celery
2   tablespoons finely chopped onion
2   tablespoons parsley flakes
$^1/_4$ teaspoon salt
$^1/_8$ teaspoon oregano, crushed
$^1/_8$ teaspoon freshly ground pepper
$^1/_3$ cup sliced almonds
2   tablespoons butter or margarine, melted

SERVES: 6

Grilling Time: 10 to 12 minutes

2   *pounds swordfish steaks,*
      1 inch thick
1/2 *cup orange juice*
1/2 *cup soy sauce*
1/4 *cup ketchup*
1/4 *cup chopped parsley*
2   *tablespoons lemon juice*
2   *cloves garlic, minced*
1   *teaspoon oregano, crushed*
1   *teaspoon freshly ground*
      pepper
1/2 *teaspoon dry mustard*

SERVES: 6

Barbecued Swordfish Steak

Place steaks in baking dish. In small bowl, combine remaining ingredients; mix well. Pour marinade over steaks. Cover; refrigerate 4 hours, turning occasionally.

Remove cooking grids from grill. Preheat grill on high 5 minutes; turn controls to medium-low. Return grids to grill.

Drain steaks, reserving marinade. Brush Broiler Basket with oil. Arrange steaks in basket; place on grids. Close grill top; grill steaks 5 to 6 minutes on each side or until fish flakes easily with fork, occasionally brushing with marinade.

Cod, halibut, or salmon may be substituted for swordfish. Steaks may be grilled directly on grids without the basket.

Grilling Time: 10 to 12 minutes

1 1/2 *pounds salmon steaks, 1 inch*
       thick
1   *cup dry white wine*
1/2 *cup soy sauce*
1   *large clove garlic, minced*
1   *tablespoon Dijon mustard*

SERVES: 4 to 5

Cod, halibut, orange roughy, sole, or turbot may be substituted for salmon.

Marinated Salmon Steaks

Arrange steaks in baking dish. In small bowl, combine remaining ingredients; mix well. Pour marinade over steaks. Cover; refrigerate 1 hour, turning occasionally.

Remove cooking grids from grill. Preheat grill on high 5 minutes; turn controls to medium-low. Return grids to grill; brush with oil.

Drain steaks, reserving marinade; arrange steaks on grids. Close grill top; grill steaks 5 to 6 minutes on each side or until fish flakes easily with fork, occasionally brushing with marinade.

Grilling Time: 10 to 12 minutes

2   *pounds tuna steaks, 1 inch*
      thick
1/2 *cup dry sherry or apple juice*
1/4 *cup soy sauce*
2   *tablespoons lemon juice*
2   *tablespoons minced onion*
1   *tablespoon grated gingerroot*
1   *tablespoon vegetable oil*
1/4 *teaspoon freshly ground*
      pepper

SERVES: 6

Cod, halibut, haddock, salmon, and swordfish steaks may be substituted for tuna. Steaks may be grilled in a Thermos® Broiler Basket, that has been brushed with oil.

Tuna Teriyaki

Arrange steaks in baking dish. In small saucepan, combine remaining ingredients; heat thoroughly over low heat. Cool slightly; pour marinade over steaks. Cover; refrigerate 2 hours, turning occasionally.

Remove cooking grids from grill. Preheat grill on high 5 minutes; turn controls to medium-low. Return grids to grill; brush with oil.

Drain steaks, reserving marinade; arrange steaks on grids. Close grill top; grill steaks 5 to 6 minutes on each side or until fish flakes easily with fork, occasionally brushing with marinade.

Savory Salmon Steaks

Arrange salmon steaks in baking dish. In small bowl, combine remaining ingredients; mix well. Pour marinade over steaks. Cover; refrigerate 2 hours, turning occasionally.

Remove cooking grids from grill. Preheat grill on high 5 minutes; turn controls to medium-low. Return grids to grill; brush with oil.

Drain steaks, reserving marinade; arrange steaks on grids. Close grid top; grill steaks 5 to 6 minutes on each side or until fish flakes easily with fork, occasionally brushing with marinade.

Grilling Time: 10 to 12 minutes

1   pound salmon steaks, 1 inch thick
1/4 cup Italian dressing
1   tablespoon chopped parsley
1/4 teaspoon minced onion
1   teaspoon lemon-pepper seasoning

SERVES: 2 to 3

Cod, haddock, or halibut steaks may be substituted for salmon.

Sesame Sea Bass

Rinse fish; pat dry with paper towels. Sprinkle cavity of fish with lemon juice. Brush skin with butter; sprinkle with pepper. Coat with sesame seed. Reserve remaining butter and sesame seed.

Remove cooking grids from grill. Preheat grill on high 5 minutes; turn controls to low. Return grids to grill.

Brush Fish Broiler with oil; arrange fish in broiler. Place on grids. Close grill top; grill fish 10 to 12 minutes on each side or until fish flakes easily with fork. During last 4 minutes, brush with butter and sprinkle with sesame seed.

Grilling Time: 24 to 30 minutes

1   2-to 3-pound dressed whole sea bass
2   tablespoons lemon juice
1/2 cup butter or margarine, melted
1/4 teaspoon freshly ground pepper
1/2 cup sesame seed, toasted

SERVES: 4 to 6

Striped bass, salmon, trout, pike, or red snapper may be substituted for sea bass.

Mackerel Steaks

Arrange steaks on large sheet of heavy-duty foil; turn up sides 1 inch. In small skillet, sauté green pepper and onion in butter until vegetables are crisp-tender. Stir in ketchup, lemon pepper, and bay leaf. Cover; cook 5 minutes, stirring occasionally. Discard bay leaf. Cool slightly. Spoon sauce over steaks.

Remove cooking grids from grill. Preheat grill on high 5 minutes; turn controls to medium-low. Return grids to grill.

Carefully place foil with steaks on grids. Close grill top; grill steaks 5 to 6 minutes on each side, or until fish flakes easily with fork.

Grilling Time: 10 to 12 minutes

1 1/2 pounds mackerel steaks, 1 inch thick
1/2   cup chopped green pepper
1/2   cup chopped onion
2   tablespoons butter or margarine
1/2   cup ketchup
1/4   teaspoon lemon-pepper seasoning
1   bay leaf

SERVES: 4 to 5

Haddock, halibut, or swordfish may be substituted for mackerel.

Grilling Time: 20 to 30 minutes

- 1   4-pound dressed whole red fish
- 2   tablespoons butter or margarine, melted
- 2   tablespoons vegetable oil
- 1   tablespoon paprika
- 1   teaspoon oregano, crushed
- 1   teaspoon thyme, crushed
- 1/2   teaspoon freshly ground black pepper
- 1/2   teaspoon cayenne pepper
- 1/4   teaspoon onion powder
- 1/4   teaspoon salt

SERVES: 4

Grilling Time: 6 to 8 minutes

- 1/2   cup vegetable oil
- 2   tablespoons white wine vinegar
- 2   tablespoons finely chopped fresh mint
- 1/4   teaspoon freshly ground pepper
- 1/8   teaspoon hot pepper sauce
- 1/8   teaspoon salt
- 2   pounds sea scallops

SERVES: 4 to 6

SHRIMP & DILL: Substitute 2 pounds shelled, deveined, large shrimp for scallops. Omit vinegar and mint; add 1/4 cup dry white wine and 1/4 teaspoon dill weed.

Grilling Time: 6 to 8 minutes

- 1/4   cup sliced green onions
- 1   clove garlic, minced (optional)
- 1/4   teaspoon dry mustard
- 1/8   teaspoon lemon-pepper seasoning
- 2   tablespoons butter or margarine
- 1   pound sea scallops
      Hot cooked rice

SERVES: 2 to 3

Cajun Redfish

Rinse fish; pat dry with paper towels. In small bowl, combine remaining ingredients; mix well.

Remove cooking grids from grill. Preheat grill on high 5 minutes; turn controls to medium-low. Return grids to grill; brush with oil.

Brush fish with butter mixture; place fish on grids. Close grill top; grill fish 10 to 15 minutes on each side, occasionally brushing with butter mixture.

Red snapper, sea bass, trout, or whitefish may be substituted for red fish.

Whole fish can be grilled in a Thermos® Fish Broiler that has been brushed with oil.

Freshly Minted Scallops

In large bowl, combine all ingredients, except scallops; mix well. Add scallops; mix lightly. Cover; refrigerate 2 hours.

Remove cooking grids from grill. Preheat grill on high 5 minutes; turn controls to medium. Return grids to grill; brush with oil.

Drain scallops, reserving marinade; thread scallops onto long metal skewers. Arrange kabobs on grids; brush with marinade. Close grill top; grill kabobs 6 to 8 minutes or until scallops are opaque, occasionally turning and brushing with marinade.

Savory Scallops

Remove cooking grids from grill. Preheat grill on high 5 minutes; turn controls to medium. Return grids to grill.

In large skillet on grids, sauté onions, garlic, mustard, and lemon pepper in butter 3 minutes. Add scallops; sauté 3 to 5 minutes or until opaque. Serve on rice.

SAUTÉED SHRIMP: Substitute 1 pound shelled, deveined shrimp for scallops. Omit garlic; add 1/4 teaspoon oregano, crushed.

SCALLOPS A LA CREME: Just before serving, stir in 1/4 cup cream and 1 teaspoon dry sherry; heat thoroughly.

Barbecued Shrimp

In large bowl, combine all ingredients, except shrimp; mix well. Add shrimp; mix lightly. Divide shrimp among 6 squares of heavy-duty foil. Bring together four corners of each square; twist to close packets.

Remove cooking grids from grill. Preheat grill on high 5 minutes; turn controls to low. Return grids to grill.

Arrange foil packets on grids. Close grill top; grill 6 to 8 minutes or until shrimp are opaque.

Grilling Time: 6 to 8 minutes

- 1/3 cup butter or margarine, melted
- 3 tablespoons lemon juice
- 2 tablespoons chopped parsley
- 1 clove garlic, minced (optional)
- 1/2 teaspoon curry powder
- 1/4 teaspoon freshly ground pepper
- 1/8 teaspoon salt
- 1/8 teaspoon sugar
- 2 pounds shelled, deveined, large shrimp

SERVES: 6

Outdoor Lobster Tails

Using kitchen shears or sharp knife, remove thin membrane from meat side of tail. To prevent tail from curling, bend back shell until it cracks in several places or insert long metal skewer lengthwise between shell and meat. In small bowl, combine remaining ingredients; mix well.

Remove cooking grids from grill. Preheat grill on high 5 minutes; turn controls to medium. Return grids to grill; brush with oil.

Brush lobster meat with sauce; place tails, shell side down, on grids. Close grill top; grill tails 6 to 8 minutes. Turn; brush with sauce. Continue to grill, shell side up, 6 to 8 minutes or until lobster meat is opaque.

Grilling Time: 12 to 16 minutes

- 4 6-to 8-ounce frozen rock lobster tails, thawed
- 1/3 cup butter or margarine, melted
- 1 tablespoon lemon or lime juice
- 1/4 teaspoon cayenne pepper (optional)
- 1/8 teaspoon sugar

SERVES: 4

Hickory Smoked Salmon

Prepare wood chip log as directed (page 8). Rinse fish; pat dry with paper towels. Combine remaining ingredients, except lemon pepper; mix well. Brush fish with butter mixture; sprinkle with lemon pepper.

Remove cooking grids from grill. Move lava rocks to right side. Place drip pan opposite rocks on left side of grate; fill with water to 2-inch depth. Preheat grill on high 5 minutes.

Place wood chip log on lava rocks. Close grill top; heat on high 10 to 20 minutes or until chips begin to smolder. Turn controls to low. Using basting bulb, refill drip pan if necessary. Return grids to grill; brush left grid with oil.

Place salmon on left grid over drip pan. Close grill top; smoke salmon 2 hours or until fish flakes easily with fork, occasionally brushing with butter mixture. Add more water and wood chip logs as necessary. Cool salmon. Wrap securely in foil; refrigerate until ready to serve.

Grilling Time: 2 hours

- 1 5-to 7-pound dressed whole salmon
- 2 tablespoons butter or margarine, melted
- 2 tablespoons lemon or lime juice
- 2 tablespoons chopped dill
  Lemon-pepper seasoning

SERVES: 10 to 12

One teaspoon dill weed may be substituted for fresh dill.

A Thermos® Grill Smoker filled with soaked wood chips is an excellent alternative to the wood chip log. Refer to the directions on (page 8).

Kabobs, kebobs, shish-kabobs, sis kebabs, brochettes, pinchos, or sates . . . no matter what the language, barbecuing on skewers is one of the most attractive ways of preparing and serving food. It's a culinary art form! What is more appealing than a splendid array of skewered meats, vegetables, and fruit sizzling on the grill. Almost any food of reasonable size and firmness can be "shished." For serious kabobbers, here are a few tips to streamline your style:

- Select fresh foods that are compatible in color, flavor, and firmness. Alternate foods of various colors on each skewer. Foods must be firm enough to remain on a skewer even after they have finished cooking. This is especially important when using canned or precooked foods.

- To reduce grilling time, microwave or parboil very firm foods, such as carrots, potatoes, and whole onions, before threading onto skewers.

- Cut foods in a variety of shapes that are similar in size so they will grill in about the same length of time. If there is a definite difference in size or cooking time, thread the foods onto separate skewers.

- Marinate foods, if desired, before threading onto skewers. Foods that will be arranged on the same skewers should be marinated in the same sauce.

A Thermos® Shish-Kabob Set, with six 12-inch skewers and a raised rack, makes it easier to turn kabobs during grilling.

Ham & Pineapple Kabobs

Grilling Time: 8 minutes

1	*16-ounce can pineapple chunks*
1/4	*cup butter or margarine*
2	*tablespoons brown sugar*
1/2	*teaspoon curry powder*
1/4	*teaspoon dry mustard*
1	*pound fully-cooked ham,*
	cut into 1-inch cubes
2	*pears, cut into wedges*

SERVES: 4

Drain pineapple, reserving juice. In small saucepan, combine 1/2 cup juice, butter, sugar, curry powder, and mustard; heat, stirring constantly, over medium heat until sugar dissolves.

Remove cooking grids from grill. Preheat grill on high 5 minutes; turn controls to medium. Return grids to grill; brush with oil.

Alternately thread ham and fruit onto long metal skewers; brush with sauce. Arrange kabobs on grids. Close grill top; grill kabobs 8 minutes or until hot, frequently brushing with sauce.

Polynesian Beef

Place beef in baking dish. In small bowl, combine remaining ingredients; mix well. Pour marinade over beef. Cover; refrigerate 2 hours, turning occasionally.

Remove cooking grids from grill. Preheat grill on high 5 minutes; turn controls to medium. Return grids to grill; brush with oil.

Drain beef, reserving marinade; thread beef onto metal skewers. Arrange kabobs on grids. Close grill top; grill kabobs 8 to 10 minutes or to desired doneness, occasionally turning and brushing with marinade.

2 *pounds beef top round or sirloin steak, cut into 1 1/2-inch cubes*
3/4 *cup soy sauce*
1/4 *cup sweet sherry*
1/4 *cup honey*
1 *tablespoon vegetable oil*
2 *cloves garlic, minced*
2 *tablespoons minced fresh ginger*
1/2 *teaspoon cinnamon*
1/4 *teaspoon ground cloves*

SERVES: 8

Veal and Vegetable Kabobs

Place veal in baking dish. In small bowl, combine wine, ketchup, oil, basil, salt, and ground pepper; mix well. Pour over meat. Cover; refrigerate 2 hours, turning occasionally.

Remove cooking grids from grill. Preheat grill on high 5 minutes; turn controls to medium. Return grids to grill; brush with oil.

Drain veal, reserving marinade. Thread veal, mushrooms, peppers, and tomatoes onto separate, long, metal skewers. Arrange kabobs, except tomatoes, on grids; brush with marinade.

Close grill top; grill kabobs 8 to 10 minutes or until meat is tender and vegetables are crisp-tender, occasionally turning and brushing with marinade. During last 2 minutes, grill tomatoes, brushing once with marinade.

Grilling Time: 8 to 10 minutes

1 1/2 *pounds boneless veal, cut into 1-inch cubes*
1/2 *cup dry white wine*
1/4 *cup ketchup*
2 *tablespoons vegetable oil*
1/2 *teaspoon basil, crushed*
1/2 *teaspoon salt*
1/8 *teaspoon freshly ground pepper*
12 *large fresh mushroom caps*
2 *green peppers, cut into 1-inch squares*
12 *firm cherry tomatoes*

SERVES: 4 to 6

Beef Sate

Place beef and red peppers in baking dish. In small bowl, combine coconut milk, onions, juice, oil, and chili pepper; mix well. Pour marinade over beef and peppers. Cover; refrigerate 1 hour, turning occasionally.

Remove cooking grids from grill. Preheat grill on high 5 minutes; turn controls to medium. Return grids to grill; brush with oil.

Drain beef and red peppers, reserving marinade; alternately thread beef, peppers, and orange sections onto long metal skewers. Arrange kabobs on grids.

Close grill top; grill kabobs 8 to 10 minutes or to desired doneness, occasionally turning and brushing with sauce. To serve, remove beef, peppers, and orange sections from skewers; sprinkle with sesame seed.

For an easy dipping sauce, blend 1/3 cup peanut butter with 1/4 cup honey or pineapple preserves, 1/4 cup dairy sour cream, and 1/2 teaspoon grated gingerroot or 1/4 teaspoon ground ginger.

Grilling Time: 8 to 10 minutes

2 *pounds boneless beef or veal, cut into 1 1/2-inch cubes*
2 *sweet red peppers, cut into 1 1/2-inch squares*
1/2 *cup coconut milk or sweet white wine*
1/2 *cup minced onions*
1/4 *cup lime juice*
2 *tablespoons vegetable oil*
1 *tablespoon chopped green chili pepper*
2 *navel oranges, peeled and sectioned*
1 *tablespoon sesame seed, toasted*

SERVES: 6

Grilling Time: 12 to 15 minutes

1/4	cup chili sauce
1/4	cup horseradish mustard
2	tablespoons vegetable oil
2	tablespoons water
2	tablespoons chili powder
1/2	teaspoon oregano, crushed
6	precooked smoked kielbasa, cut into thirds
1	16-ounce can whole potatoes, drained
2	green peppers, cut into 1-inch squares
4	ears corn, cleaned and cut into 2-inch pieces
1/4	cup butter or margarine, melted
	Freshly ground pepper

SERVES: 4

Kielbasabobs

In small bowl, combine chili sauce, mustard, oil, water, chili powder, and oregano; mix well.

Remove cooking grids from grill. Preheat grill on high 5 minutes; turn controls to low. Return grids to grill; brush with oil.

Thread meat, potatoes, green peppers, and corn onto separate, long, metal skewers. Brush vegetables with butter; sprinkle with pepper. Arrange kabobs on grids.

Close grill top; grill kabobs 12 to 15 minutes, or until sausage is hot and vegetables are crisp-tender, frequently turning kabobs. During last 10 minutes, occasionally brush meat with sauce. Serve meat with remaining sauce.

Grilling Time: 12 to 15 minutes

2	pounds boneless pork, cut into 1 1/2-inch cubes
1/2	cup strong coffee
1/4	cup dry red wine
2	tablespoons cider vinegar
2	tablespoons soy sauce
1	teaspoon sugar
1/2	teaspoon rosemary, crushed
1/2	teaspoon tarragon, crushed
1/4	teaspoon freshly ground pepper
2	apples, cut into 1-inch cubes
1/4	cup orange juice

SERVES: 6

Spicy Pork Kabobs

Place meat in baking dish. In small bowl, combine remaining ingredients, except apples and orange juice; mix well. Pour over meat. Cover; refrigerate 2 hours, turning occasionally.

Remove cooking grids from grill. Preheat grill on high 5 minutes; turn controls to medium. Return grids to grill; brush with oil.

Drain meat, reserving marinade. Thread meat and apples onto separate, long, metal skewers; brush apples with orange juice. Arrange meat kabobs on grids.

Close grill top; grill kabobs 12 to 15 minutes or to desired doneness, occasionally turning and brushing with marinade. During last 4 minutes, grill apple kabobs, occasionally brushing with orange juice.

PORK & FRUIT KABOBS: Drain one 16-ounce can pineapple chunks, reserving 1/2 cup juice. Substitute juice for red wine; omit tarragon. Alternately thread pineapple chunks and apples on skewers.

Grilling Time: 6 to 8 minutes

1/4	cup vegetable oil
2	tablespoons lemon juice
1	teaspoon oregano, crushed
1/8	teaspoon freshly ground pepper
1/8	teaspoon salt
2	pounds shelled, deveined, large shrimp
1	medium zucchini, cut diagonally into 1/4-inch slices

SERVES: 6 to 8

Shrimp Italiano

In large bowl, combine all ingredients, except shrimp and zucchini; mix well. Add shrimp; mix lightly. Cover; refrigerate 2 hours.

Remove cooking grids from grill. Preheat grill on high 5 minutes; turn controls to low. Return grids to grill; brush with oil.

Drain shrimp, reserving marinade; alternately thread shrimp and zucchini onto long metal skewers. Arrange kabobs on grids; brush with marinade. Close grill top; grill kabobs 6 to 8 minutes or until shrimp is opaque, occasionally brushing with marinade.

Cod Kabobs

In small saucepan, combine butter, dill, pepper, and cayenne; heat thoroughly over low heat.

Remove cooking grids from grill. Preheat grill on high 5 minutes; turn controls to medium. Return grids to grill; brush with oil.

Alternately thread cod and green peppers onto long metal skewers and tomatoes onto separate skewer; brush with sauce. Arrange cod and pepper kabobs on grids. Close grill top; grill kabobs 15 to 20 minutes or until fish flakes easily with fork, occasionally brushing with sauce. During last 5 minutes, grill tomatoes, occasionally brushing with sauce.

- 1/2 cup butter or margarine
- 1 teaspoon dill weed
- 1/4 teaspoon freshly ground pepper
- 1/8 teaspoon cayenne pepper
- 1/2 pound partially frozen cod steaks, cut into 1-inch cubes
- 2 large green peppers, cut into 1-inch squares
- 12 cherry tomatoes

SERVES: 4 to 6

Halibut, shark, swordfish, or tuna steaks may be substituted for cod.

Fruit Kabobs

In small saucepan, combine honey, butter, and juice; heat thoroughly over low heat.

Remove cooking grids from grill. Preheat grill on high 5 minutes; turn controls to low. Return grids to grill; brush with oil.

Alternately thread fruit onto long metal skewers; brush with sauce. Arrange kabobs on grids. Close grill top; grill kabobs 10 to 12 minutes or until hot, frequently turning and brushing with sauce.

Firm fruit (apples, apricots, bananas, nectarines, oranges, peaches, pears, pineapple, and plums) are ideal for kabobs.

- 1 cup honey
- 1/4 cup butter or margarine
- 1 1/2 tablespoons lemon juice
- 3 cups assorted fresh or canned fruit, cut into desired shapes.

SERVES: 6

Lemon or vanilla yogurt or dairy sour cream sweetened with honey may be served as a dipping sauce for the kabobs.

Vegetable Kabobs

In small saucepan, combine butter, lemon pepper, and salt; heat thoroughly over low heat.

Remove cooking grids from grill. Preheat grill on high 5 minutes; turn controls to medium. Return grids to grill; brush with oil.

Alternately thread onions, mushrooms, zucchini, and green pepper onto separate, long, metal skewers; brush with sauce. Arrange kabobs on grids. Close grill top; grill kabobs 15 to 20 minutes or until vegetables are crisp-tender, occasionally turning and brushing with sauce.

- 1/4 cup butter or margarine
- 1/4 teaspoon lemon-pepper seasoning
- 1/4 teaspoon salt
- 8 small onions, parboiled
- 8 large fresh mushroom caps
- 2 small zucchini, cut diagonally into 1-inch pieces
- 1 green pepper, cut into 1-inch squares

SERVES: 4

Many other vegetables can be substituted for the ones in this recipe. If a vegetable is quite firm, it should be parboiled before threading onto skewers.

FESTIVE FRUITS AND VEGETABLES

Fruits and vegetables are the decorative accompaniments that add color, variety, and style to any outdoor meal. Whether fresh, frozen, or canned, most fruits and vegetables can be cooked or heated on a gas grill. Depending on the size and firmness, they can be grilled directly on the grids, steamed in foil packets, or barbecued on skewers. In the "Sauces, Marinades, & More!" chapter (pages 13-15) you will find many compatible sauces and seasoned butters, such as Dijon Mustard Sauce, Dill Cream Sauce, Curry Butter, and Parsley Lemon Butter. The "Colorful Kabobs" chapter (pages 82-85) also offers several suggestions and recipes for grilling fruits and vegetables on skewers . . . with or without meat, poultry, or seafood.

If you have been missing the marvelous potential of fruits and vegetables on the grill, here are a few introductory tips:

- Allow $1/2$ to $2/3$ cup or $1/4$ to $1/3$ pound per serving.

- To reduce grilling time, microwave or parboil firm vegetables like potatoes, carrots, and cauliflower before grilling.

- Use the indirect method or the direct method (page 7) with a medium to low setting for most fruits and vegetables.

- When grilling in foil, use "drugstore wrap" packets for fruits and vegetables with a low moisture content. This makes turning easy. Use the "pouch" technique for foods with a high moisture content.

- To make **Foil Packets**, place food in the center of a sheet of heavy-duty foil and top with butter, seasonings, or sauces. Bring together long sides of foil; then double fold sides and ends of foil. For **Foil Pouches**, bring together the four corners of the foil sheet; then fold or twist. To seal sides, fold over and press against the pouch. Do not turn the pouch during grilling.

- Use a single thickness of heavy-duty foil for most foods. The foil sheet should be approximately triple the size of the area covered by the food.

- For extra moisture, add 1 to 3 ice cubes to foil packets or pouches before sealing.

- To prevent piercing the foil, turn packets with tongs.

- Wrap whole or large pieces of fruit or vegetables individually in foil.

- Grill frozen vegetables in foil packets over medium heat for about 40 to 50 minutes or until thoroughly heated. To hasten grilling time, slightly thaw the vegetables to separate the pieces.

To prepare the gas grill, remove cooking grids. Preheat the grill on high for 5 minutes; then turn controls to medium or low, as indicated in the recipe. Return the grids to the grill. If the fruit or vegetable is to be grilled directly on the grids, brush the grids with oil. Arrange the food on the grids and grill with the grill top closed.

ON THE GRIDS

Prepare the following fresh fruits and vegetables as indicated. Grill the food directly on the grids, without foil, over low to medium heat for the length of time specified or until tender. Grilling times may vary, depending on the degree of ripeness and the initial temperature of the fruits and vegetables. Amounts serve four people.

FRUIT

Bananas: Halve 2 large firm bananas lengthwise, leaving peel intact; brush cut surfaces with honey. Grill over low heat 6 to 8 minutes, frequently turning and brushing with honey.

Cantaloupe: Halve 1 medium cantaloupe lengthwise. Remove seeds; peel. Cut crosswise into 1-inch slices. Brush with a combination of 2 tablespoons each melted butter or margarine and honey and 1 tablespoon lemon or lime juice. Grill over medium heat 4 to 6 minutes, frequently turning and brushing with butter mixture.

Grapefruit: Halve 2 medium grapefruit. Brush cut surfaces with a combination of 2 tablespoons melted butter or margarine and brown sugar and $1/2$ teaspoon ground ginger. Grill over medium heat 10 to 12 minutes, frequently turning and brushing with butter mixture.

Pineapple: Peel and core 1 medium pineapple; cut into 8 wedges. Brush with a combination of $1/2$ cup orange juice, 2 tablespoons brown sugar, and 1 tablespoon rum or orange liqueur. Grill over medium heat 6 to 8 minutes, frequently turning and brushing with sauce. Top pineapple with dairy sour cream or vanilla yogurt.

VEGETABLES

Eggplant: Cut 1 large eggplant crosswise into $3/4$-inch slices. Brush with melted butter or margarine; sprinkle with grated Parmesan cheese and lemon-pepper seasoning. Grill over medium heat 20 to 25 minutes, turning frequently.

Green, Red, or Yellow Peppers: Quarter 2 peppers; remove seeds and membrane. Brush inside of peppers with a combination of 2 tablespoons melted butter or margarine, $1/4$ teaspoon Italian herb seasonings, and $1/8$ teaspoon cayenne pepper. Grill over medium heat 10 to 15 minutes or until crisp-tender.

Grilled Potatoes (sweet or white): Brush 4 medium unpeeled potatoes with melted margarine. Grill over medium heat 50 to 60 minutes, turning occasionally.

Potatoes Slices: Cut 3 large russet potatoes into $1/4$-inch slices. Brush with a combination of $1/4$ cup melted butter or margarine and $1/4$ teaspoon each freshly ground pepper and salt or garlic salt. Grill over medium heat 10 minutes or until tender, frequently turning and brushing with butter mixture. For variety, omit butter and seasonings; brush potatoes with Italian dressing; sprinkle with grated Parmesan cheese.

Tomatoes: Halve 4 medium tomatoes crosswise. Brush with a combination of 2 tablespoons melted butter or margarine and $1/4$ teaspoon dill weed or crushed basil, oregano, or rosemary. Grill over low heat 8 to 10 minutes, turning frequently and brushing with butter mixture.

Zucchini: Halve 4 small zucchini lengthwise. Brush cut surfaces with 2 tablespoons melted butter or margarine and $1/2$ teaspoon Italian herb seasoning. Grill over medium heat 20 to 25 minutes, turning frequently and brushing with butter mixture. Sprinkle with shredded Cheddar or mozzarella cheese.

ALL WRAPPED UP

Prepare and grill the following fruit, vegetable, or combinations in foil packets or pouches (page 86), as directed or until tender. Amounts serve 4 people.

FRUIT

Stuffed Apples: Core 4 medium apples; fill centers with brown sugar and chopped walnuts. Wrap each in foil. Grill over medium heat 20 to 25 minutes, turning occasionally.

Curried Peaches: Peel and halve 4 medium peaches; remove pits. Fill centers with 1 teaspoon each butter or margarine and honey; sprinkle with curry powder. Grill foil packet over medium heat 12 to 15 minutes, turning occasionally. Serve with dairy sour cream or vanilla yogurt.

Stuffed Pears: Peel and core 4 medium pears; fill centers with butterscotch or caramel topping. Grill foil packet over low heat 10 to 15 minutes. Serve with yogurt or whipped cream.

Plums: Halve 4 large purple or red plums; remove pits. Top each half with 1/2 teaspoon each butter or margarine and brown sugar. Grill foil pouch over medium heat 12 to 15 minutes.

VEGETABLES

Asparagus: Dot 1 pound asparagus spears with butter or margarine; sprinkle with sliced almonds. Grill foil packet over medium heat 15 to 20 minutes, turning occasionally.

Cherry Tomatoes & Patty Pan Squash: Combine 1 1/2 cups cherry tomatoes, 1 cup baby patty pan squash, halved, and 1/4 cup sliced green onions. Dot with 2 tablespoons butter or margarine; sprinkle with crushed basil leaves or dill weed and freshly ground pepper. Grill foil pouch over low heat 15 to 20 minutes.

Corn-On-The-Cob: Pull back husks of 4 ears of corn; remove silk. Replace husks around corn. With string or strips of husk, tie husks to corn in two or three places. Let soak in water for 15 to 20 minutes; drain. Brush husks with melted butter or margarine. Wrap in foil. Grill over medium heat 20 to 25 minutes, turning every 5 minutes. Serve with butter, freshly ground pepper, and salt.

Mushrooms: Slice or halve 1/2 pound fresh mushrooms; dot with 2 tablespoons butter or margarine. Sprinkle with 2 tablespoons chopped parsley and 1/4 teaspoon freshly ground pepper. Grill foil pouch over low heat 10 to 12 minutes. For variety, add 2 green onions, sliced, before grilling. Sprinkle with grated Parmesan cheese before serving.

Onions: Cut 2 medium onions into thick slices. Dot with butter or margarine; sprinkle with Italian seasonings. Grill foil pouch over low heat 20 to 25 minutes. Sprinkle with shredded Cheddar cheese.

Stuffed Russets: Brush 4 medium russet potatoes with melted butter or margarine; wrap each potato in foil. Grill over medium heat 50 to 60 minutes. Serve with a selection of toppings, such as shredded cheese, dairy sour cream, finely chopped onion or green pepper, crisp diced bacon, and chopped olives.

Zucchini & Tomatoes: Combine 2 small zucchini, sliced, and 2 medium tomatoes, chopped. Sprinkle with 3 tablespoons grated Parmesan cheese, 1/2 teaspoon crushed oregano, and 1/4 teaspoon salt; dot with 2 tablespoons margarine. Grill foil packet over low heat 15 to 20 minutes.

SKEWERED FOR SUCCESS

Kabobs are especially effective for small fruits and vegetables. Check the "Colorful Kabobs" chapter (pages 82-85) for helpful tips on assembling skewered foods and for a variety of kabob ideas. Here are a few additional suggestions. Thread any of the following fruit or vegetable combinations onto long metal skewers and grill on the grids for the length of time indicated or until tender. A Thermos® Shish-Kabob Set with skewers and a rack is ideal for "kabobbing."

Summer Squash: Thread onto skewers 1/4-inch slices green and yellow zucchini and baby patty pan squash, halved. Brush with melted butter or margarine; sprinkle with lemon-pepper seasoning and cayenne pepper. Grill over low heat 15 to 20 minutes, occasionally turning and brushing with butter.

Mushrooms, Tomatoes, & Zucchini: Thread onto skewers medium mushroom caps, cherry tomatoes, and thinly sliced zucchini. Brush with melted butter or margarine; sprinkle with dill weed and freshly ground pepper. Grill over low heat 10 to 12 minutes, occasionally turning and brushing with butter.

Whether skewered and cooked directly on the grill (left) or prepared with a Thermos® Shish Kabob Set (right), vegetable kabobs give flare to any outdoor meal.

New Potatoes, Peppers, & Onions: Cook and peel new potatoes; thread onto skewers with 1-inch squares of green or red peppers, and onion wedges. Brush with Italian dressing or White Wine Marinade (page 14); sprinkle with freshly ground pepper or curry powder. Grill over medium heat 15 to 20 minutes, occasionally turning and brushing with dressing.

Melon & Plums: Thread onto skewers cubes of cantaloupe or honeydew melon and wedges of purple or red plums. Brush with lemon or lime juice and honey. Grill over low heat 4 to 6 minutes, frequently turning and brushing with honey.

Apples & Pears: Thread onto skewers wedges of apples and pears. Brush with melted butter or margarine and maple-flavored syrup. Grill over low heat 8 to 10 minutes, frequently turning and brushing with butter and syrup.

APPETIZERS,

SNACKS,

ETC.

From party appetizers and heartier snacks to savory hot breads, this chapter offers a few select favorites to stimulate your appetite and imagination. Meal starters such as Barbecued Chicken Wings (below) and Beef Teriyaki Appetizers (below) can convert to main course status by simply increasing the serving size. The Super Submarine (page 92) may be varied by substituting other cooked meats, cheese, and condiments for the ingredients suggested in the recipe. Layered sandwiches provide great flexibility and an excellent opportunity to reuse tasty leftovers. All of the seasoned breads may be completely prepared and wrapped a day or two in advance and refrigerated until grilling time. Add a few more minutes to the heating time if the bread is cold.

Barbecued Chicken Wings

Grilling Time: 15 to 20 minutes

Cut chicken wings into 3 pieces at joints; discard tips. Arrange wings in baking dish. In small bowl, combine remaining ingredients, except paprika; mix well. Pour marinade over wings. Cover; refrigerate 4 hours, turning occasionally.

Remove cooking grids from grill. Preheat grill on high 5 minutes; turn controls to medium. Return grids to grill; brush with oil.

Drain wings, reserving marinade; sprinkle with paprika. Arrange wings on grids. Close grill top; grill wings 15 to 20 minutes, occasionally turning and brushing with marinade.

  2   *pounds chicken wings*
 $1/4$ *cup apple or pineapple juice*
 $1/4$ *cup dry white wine*
  2   *tablespoons honey*
  2   *tablespoons soy sauce*
  1   *teaspoon curry powder*
 $1/4$ *teaspoon ground ginger*
 $1/4$ *teaspoon salt*
      Paprika

SERVES: 8

Beef Teriyaki Appetizers

Grilling Time: 5 to 8 minutes

Place meat in large bowl. In small bowl, combine remaining ingredients; mix well. Pour over meat. Cover; refrigerate 2 hours, turning occasionally.

Remove cooking grids from grill. Preheat grill on high 5 minutes; turn controls to medium. Return grids to grill; brush with oil.

Drain meat, reserving marinade. Thread meat onto long metal skewers; arrange kabobs on grids. Close grill top; grill kabobs 5 to 8 minutes, occasionally turning and brushing with marinade. Remove meat from skewers; serve on toothpicks.

  2   *pounds beef top round or*
      sirloin, cut into 1-inch cubes
 $1/2$ *cup dry sherry*
 $1/3$ *cup soy sauce*
  2   *tablespoons brown sugar*
  1   *teaspoon grated gingerroot*
  1   *clove garlic, minced (optional)*

SERVES: 8

A Thermos® Shish Kabob Set that includes 6 metal skewers and a raised rack is ideal for "kabobbing." It makes turning the kabobs easier and helps the food to retain its shape.

←**Melon and Plums (page 89),**
   Barbecued Shrimp (page 79),
   Barbecued Chicken Wings (above),
   Hot Buttered Brie (page 92)

Grilling Time: 10 to 15 minutes

1 1-pound wheel Brie cheese
2 tablespoons butter or margarine,
    softened
1 cup sliced almonds, lightly
    toasted
    Thinly sliced French bread or
    assorted crackers

SERVES: 8 to 10

Hot Buttered Brie

Spread top of cheese with butter; sprinkle with nuts. Place in heatproof dish or foil pan.

Remove cooking grids from grill. Preheat grill on high 5 minutes; turn left control to off and right control to low. Return grids to grill.

Place cheese on left grid. Close grill top; grill cheese 10 to 15 minutes.

BRIE & CHUTNEY: Omit butter; spread top of cheese with ³/₄ cup apricot or mango chutney or apricot preserves. Garnish with nuts.

Grilling Time: 14 to 18 minutes

1 1-pound loaf Vienna bread
¹/₂ cup butter or margarine,
    softened
2 tablespoons horseradish
    mustard
8 ounces thinly-sliced baked or
    boiled ham
8 ounces Cheddar or Swiss
    cheese slices
4 ounces thinly-sliced cooked
    chicken or turkey
1 small onion, thinly sliced
1 green pepper, cut into thin
    rings
1 cup alfalfa sprouts

SERVES: 4

Super Submarine

Remove cooking grids from grill. Preheat grill on high 5 minutes; turn controls to medium. Return grids to grill.

Cut bread lengthwise into halves; spread cut sides of bread with butter. Arrange bread, cut side down, on grids. Close grill top; grill bread 2 to 3 minutes or until lightly toasted. Turn controls to low.

Spread toasted bread with mustard; layer remaining ingredients on bottom half of bread. Cover with top half. Wrap sandwich securely in double thickness of heavy-duty foil; place sandwich on grids. Close grill top; grill sandwich 12 to 15 minutes or until cheese is melted. Cut into 4 servings.

TURKEY HOAGIE: Omit ham and mustard; increase turkey to 12 ounces. Spread toasted bread with thousand island dressing.

PASTRAMI HERO: Omit chicken and sprouts; substitute 8 ounces sliced pastrami for ham. Add 1 large tomato, thinly sliced.

Grilling Time: 18 to 20 minutes

1 frozen pizza

SERVES: 4 (12-inch pizza)
        6 (14-inch pizza)

Backyard Pizza

Remove cooking grids from grill. Preheat grill on high 5 minutes; turn controls to medium. Return grids to grill.

Remove wrapper and cardboard from frozen pizza; place on sheet of heavy-duty foil on grids. Close grill top; grill pizza 18 to 20 minutes or as directed on package for baking.

SEASONED BREADS . . . HOT OFF THE GRILL

Long or round loaves of warm fragrant bread are the perfect accompaniment for barbecued meat, poultry, or seafood. They are very easy to prepare and can be as varied as your imagination. Following are a few suggestions for heating bread on the grill:

Start with a 1-pound loaf of unsliced bread . . . French, Italian, Vienna, pumpernickel, rye, or coarse whole-wheat. Cut the loaf into 3/4-inch to 1-inch slices almost through to the bottom crust.

Blend 1/2 cup butter or margarine, softened, with any of the ingredient combinations below. Gently separate the bread slices and spread the seasoned butter on each slice. Spread any remaining mixture on top of the loaf.

Wrap the bread in a double thickness of heavy-duty foil and heat on the grill, alongside other food that is grilling, or over medium to low heat for 15 to 20 minutes or until warm.

BLUE CHEESE BREAD: Combine 1 cup crumbled blue cheese and 2 tablespoons grated Parmesan cheese with butter; mix well.

CHEDDAR CHEESE BREAD: Combine 1 cup (4 ounces) shredded Cheddar cheese, 1 tablespoon finely chopped parsley, and 1/8 teaspoon cayenne pepper with butter; mix well.

DILL BREAD: Combine 1 teaspoon dill weed and 1/4 teaspoon dry mustard with butter; mix well.

GARLIC BREAD: Combine 2 tablespoons grated Parmesan cheese and 2 cloves garlic, minced, with butter; mix well.

HERB BREAD: Combine 2 tablespoons chopped chives and 1/2 teaspoon each crushed basil and oregano with butter, mix well.

HOT & SPICY BREAD: Combine 2 tablespoons finely chopped green onion, 1 teaspoon chili powder, and 1/4 teaspoon dry mustard; mix well.

ONION BREAD: Combine 1/2 cup finely chopped onion, 1 tablespoon prepared mustard, 1/2 teaspoon poppy seed or dill weed, and 1/8 teaspoon freshly ground pepper; mix well.

PARMESAN BREAD: Combine 1/4 cup Parmesan cheese and 1/8 teaspoon cayenne pepper with butter; mix well.

PEPPER BREAD: Combine 1/4 cup finely chopped green or red pepper, 1 tablespoon finely chopped onion, and 1/4 teaspoon crushed rosemary with butter; mix well.

SWISS ONION BREAD: Combine 1 cup (4 ounces) shredded Swiss cheese, 2 tablespoons sliced green onion, and 1/4 teaspoon tarragon with butter; mix well.

INDEX